Catching Up with Daylight

a journey to wholeness

Catching Up with Daylight

a journey to wholeness

Gail Kittleson

CATCHING UP WITH DAYLIGHT

WhiteFire Publishing
13607 Bedford Rd NE
Cumberland, MD 21502

ISBNS: 978-1-939023-12-4 (print)
978-1-939023-13-1 (digital)

INTRODUCTION

"The real voyage of discovery consists not in seeking new landscapes but in having new eyes."
~ Marcel Proust

Spiritual journeys teach us to see things in new ways. The painting of a little 1940s schoolgirl, schoolbag held behind her back as she leans against a tree, provides background for this quote in a wall hanging near my desk. She gazes through her eyeglasses at a singing bird perched on a bush. With new eyes, she ingests an everyday scene, but her student dress implies that these familiar sights have new meaning.

So it is with us, as modern people attending to God's Word. How can it be that in our earthly pilgrimage, we would experience whole perception shifts? On the other hand, why should this surprise us? Our God says, "Behold, I make all things new" (Revelation 21:5, KJV). Did we think this promise referred only to the changes we experienced as baby Christians?

In God's perspective, though we tote a schoolbag replete with lessons learned, perhaps we still qualify as beginners on the journey. We planned to "arrive." We thought by now we would attain to some degree of maturity, and so we have. But as we view our passage through new eyes, perhaps we've only rounded a couple of curves.

The road from *doing* to *being* runs over rough terrain; our jogs and bumps and outright spills in the mud play into the outcome. What matters most, we learn, is not the past or the future, but this very moment.

Can we pause for breath with a grateful heart? Have we learned to absorb more spiritual comfort and less of whatever we used to seek in the way of success or acclaim or goods? Do we finally grasp the concept of God's care for us, accept His tender consolations as our birthright, and rest in divine kindness and wisdom?

Do we listen more to God's voice and less to other messages from old rules and coping mechanisms no longer appropriate for our autonomy? Do we take risks, secure in our call to fulfill our destiny and further God's kingdom?

Do we laugh at ourselves a little more easily, take ourselves a bit less seriously, and give our feeble humanness more leeway? Can we let up on our insane expectations of perfection and let go of our severe self-judgment in order for His Spirit to use us in impossible ways? Can we sit back and allow our God to work?

Most of all, does a sense of gratitude wash over us in the morning when we wake, during times of decision, tension, distress, and hours of uncertainty? Can joy find room to run into our arms like a toddler in need of a hug?

On an early evening flight from Des Moines to Colorado Springs, a man in the seat behind me exclaimed, "We're catching up with daylight!" Surely we are, if we can answer yes to even two or three of these questions. Here's to progress, to growth, to the simplicity of coming home to ourselves. Our Lord asks in Micah's prophecy that we "walk humbly with our God."

Part One

"Here is the world. Beautiful and terrible things will happen.
Don't be afraid."
~ Frederick Buechner, American writer and theologian

August

In 2004, my Army chaplain husband Lance and I started life afresh after his fourteen-month deployment to Iraq. We had no idea the house we moved into was so hungry, and we thought we had plenty of time to rewire and refurbish the plumbing, replace old flooring, take out a couple of small walls, clean out grimy items left in closets and on shelves, and repaint before starting our jobs.

We failed to take into account the loneliness of this 125-year-old abode. Her parched bones slurped up coats and coats of primer and paint, her floorboards soaked in stain, oil, and varnish, yet cried out for more.

Getting the feel of a house takes time, first of all, to find one's way. More time is required to sense the work of light as walls come down. The space brightens, opening her lungs to breathe deeply after years of being closed to the world.

Our society takes an elementary concept for granted—houses exist for people. Several families have lived in our house, most of them members of the original family who built it in 1873. Seven brothers and sisters grew up here, in probably a third of our space. A quick tour reveals idiosyncrasies that could only come from several additions over the years. In one case an entire staircase found a new home.

My husband's small family never wanted for individual space, and although two parents and five children lived in my childhood home, our farmhouse boasted rooms galore. Human space perception differs culturally, tied to our families of origin and the communal norm. The physical area we own in this world extends into our yards or lack of them, and into our community—our town, our city, our country mile.

The first morning after moving in, even with piles of boxes

gaping at me, I went for a walk to explore this little town. Early morning mist sharpened my observation powers. Alleys invited me—I choose alley-walking whenever possible. Dirt or gravel back ways offer more interesting sights and surfaces easier on one's feet.

For a town of 1,200, this neighborhood boasts an abundance of lovely old houses with towering roofs. Not a sound reaches my ears. Even birds still sleep this morning, so it's just the houses and me. In an hour or so, people sounds will fill the air, the sun's warmth will dissipate the heavy atmospheric moisture layer, and our town's day will officially begin.

But for now, it's the quiet alleys and me: I attend to silent messages coming my way.

Light and Darkness

Sometimes I wonder about the shift from night to day. What exactly defines the difference between night and morning, darkness and light? The Apostle John encourages us to claim our status as God's children and keep our footsteps out of the shadows.

Lectio Divina, an ancient Benedictine form of meditation, invites us deep into the word *light*. From the first chapter of John's Gospel, what one word draws my attention today? After several readings, I wait. *Light* focuses my thoughts. What does the writer mean by light, and what action would God have me take concerning that meaning?

First, the context: "In Him was life, and the life was the light of the world" (NIV). I didn't get very far. Four verses. That's okay. Gone are the days of complicated, application-oriented Bible studies that tackled a whole chapter or more at a time in verse-by-verse analysis. Today I ruminate about light, and that's enough.

Jesus's life was the light of the world. How did that light affect His world? Not always met with gratitude and approval, He knew some would attempt to snuff out the flame and temporarily succeed. Yet that light has pervaded throughout the ages, down to this time in history. It's the same light that beckoned us when we first heard the Good News. Joy behooves us to remember that first light.

Sometimes darkness closes in on even God's most devout followers, as it did on our Lord. Saint John of the Cross, along with countless other ancient believers, experienced this. Saint John's sole goal—to love God—seemingly led him away from the light. We can relate to his statement: "Desolation is a file, and the endurance of great darkness is preparation for great light."

When it seems our Savior's life-giving rays flee the scene of our everyday life, we suffer a tangible sense of loss that sneaks up subtly, silently, like a snake winding its way into a camper's bedroll. Suddenly we find ourselves deep in shadow country, enveloped by a penetrating chill. Where has the light gone? What has happened to our relationship with God?

Walking in the early morning reveals gradations in atmospheric light. As a temperature change occurs with the sun's disappearance at day's end, so dawn's light streaks from the east in a vast beam, drastically changing our perceptions. Still, the precise moment when darkness becomes light escapes an astute observer. With little ado, morning comes, and with it warmth and a new day.

The atmosphere gives clues, and meteorologists work to isolate sunrise and sunset, offering precise information in their weather broadcasts. "August 27, sunrise at 5:21, sunset at 8:36."

Spiritually, I've attempted the same sort of analysis. But sometimes life moves so fast, it becomes difficult to pinpoint the appearance of light or stall the coming of darkness.

Perhaps analysis sits less well with our spiritual journeys than with meteorologists' goals. In certain seasons of life, recollected light may be enough, and we simply need to keep walking.

Fog

One early hazy morning, not another human being crossed my path during a forty-minute jaunt around town. It takes me about ten minutes to shower and throw on my jeans and a hooded fleece jacket. My husband, by nature a night owl, leaves the early mornings to me. Besides, who cares if my salt-and-pepper hair is brushed when it's still dark out?

I wandered to previously untraveled streets where most homes, like silent guards, stood tightlipped. Bicycles and children's toys supplied clues about the inhabitants, as did flower and vegetable gardens, yet mystery reigned.

But a couple of houses displayed messages for passersby. On a corner lot, a large aluminum rectangle stapled to a pole stuck into the grass read: BELIEVE ON THE LORD JESUS CHRIST AND THOU SHALT BE SAVED. Nothing to disagree with there, but the instruction rising out of the mist startled me.

Then, perhaps a rod farther, another sign directed onlookers from the side of a garage—PREPARE TO MEET THY GOD. The command led me to expect further instructions on the garage door, but no more communiqués appeared. Painted to perfection, the home displayed an impeccable yard, yet no signs of anyone living there. Maybe this structure served as a house church?

Over the course of two weeks, I pondered those signs, and rode my bike by at different hours to be sure of the contents. Each time, I saw no one. Then, in a different part of town, I spotted similar messages in front windows. Did the homeowners expect people to come to the door for further instructions after reading these curt verses?

Considering Amos 4:12 without reading the context is unthinkable, like eating a lemon versus savoring a luscious piece of lemon pie. A page-and-a-half description of the Creator's attempts to waken the Israelites, to get their attention, to encourage them to return to Yahweh precedes this injunction to prepare to meet their God.

The stark Prepare to Meet thy God wilts the spirit apart from an understanding of its cultural and historical foundations. Befuddled, we stand before this sign, not knowing how to proceed, bereft of any plan or compassionate help with a daunting, if not impossible, task.

Even comprehending the word *believe*, the other active verb in these messages, is not for the fainthearted. What does *believe* mean? How often have I verbalized belief, yet consistently proven the opposite by my actions or anxiety? Such a life-changing verb deserves to be discussed with living human beings rather than spray-painted on cold, silent manmade material.

On one location, I walked within a foot of the signs to read the fine print above and below the injunctions. What did I expect? Certainly not more imperatives, perhaps information about how to contact the sign placer, but harsh words startled me again: You Must Be Born Again. Repent and Believe the Gospel.

The fine print exuded negativity and demand. Someone with answers has decided to display them for puzzled readers, but without any interaction about the meaning and process the complicated statements invoke. If a passerby wanted to repent and believe, how would they know what the Gospel—literally, good news—entailed? How could they repent unless someone explained the ramifications? Do these messages convey life or death, hope or despair?

The next day I rode my old Schwinn bike a few miles, re-entering our community from a different direction. Lovely landscaping along a new housing area caught my eye. Suddenly, out of the flowers and bushes rose another dire aluminum warning: The Wages of Sin is Death. Once again, the statement resounds with accuracy, but the placement and tone of the message, taken out of context, certainly did nothing to encourage receptivity.

The second half of that verse declares, "...but the gift of God is eternal life through Jesus Christ our Lord." Wow! Why not include this part of the wonderful, positive message?

What bothers me most about these tender truths dismantled from their surroundings, protruding out of the ground like real estate ads, is their cumulative effect. They evoke an angry, fearsome deity, arms crossed, almost daring people to take shaky steps toward Him. For years, I trembled at the thought of that God.

Is this how believers share Scripture's answers to life's great questions? I used to think so, but what I now call "abrasive evangelism" contradicts the message itself. My perennial self-judgment once needed a legalistic system so I could know if I was "in" or "out," and I'm sure my well-intentioned witnessing seemed brash to some of my victims.

Maybe that's why these stark signs trouble me so. The more I embrace what God is doing and has done for me and all His children, the more I quake at judicious pronouncements that can do more harm than good.

Saint Francis of Assisi wrote, "Live the life. Preach the word at all times. If necessary, use words." When I first read this, I knew I'd been given food for thought that would last a good while. Does my life exude the good news that God's outrageous, proactive love invites and welcomes us, including our qualms, questions, and doubts?

The wrathful, unapproachable God evoked by these austere, impersonal signs still lurks far too close in my memory to elicit any positive sense of good news. Hopefully the theme of our home and our days lived out here will convey the mercy that has found us. We must focus on living out this message rather than spraying it on cold aluminum to shock people into compliance. We won't post any signs in our yard...but we will plant flowers.

Aqua Moon

Another morning, my teapot burbled on the stove as I searched for a pair of gloves and some fuzzy earmuffs from the white cupboard in the corner of our kitchen. We painted dark wood cabinets white to brighten this corner, and though it's small, our kitchen projects cheer.

I glanced out the window above the sink at the western sky and glimpsed an aqua moon. An aqua moon? I looked twice, and again. Yes, definitely aqua, which has never ranked as my favorite color. During town garage sale weekend, someone tried to sell me an aqua table. I thought, *How could anyone have covered good wood with this shade of paint?*

But the dawning moon, peeping tenuously from reflected pink and blue-gray just beginning to color the western sky, shone a distinct aqua. What if I had stayed in bed five minutes longer? What if I hadn't paused to heat water before heading out for my walk, and had turned down the alley facing east? I'd have missed this matchless aqua moon, never realizing that such a hue of blue-green could appear in a morning sky.

What else do I miss? Probably a lot. My mind gets set in a certain direction, not always open to innovative thoughts, unique ideas, or creative bents, though I desire an accessible, pliant attitude.

The opposite mindset, bent on control, rigidly manages everything, so nothing surprises us. What a tragic way to transact our lives! A friend recently described his family's meeting with the minister to plan their mother's funeral. The pastor asked, "What words best portray your mother's life?"

Joe exchanged a look with his brother and sister as a quiet moment passed. Then simultaneously, they all blurted out, "Control freak."

We get one fragile lifetime to earn our phrase. I don't want my children to experience a control freak mother. Each day holds a menagerie of potential surprises, and I'd hate to miss any of them, but control goes against that grain.

What if we could let go of attempts to control the great wave of joys and delights, sorrows and challenges that attend our journey? What if we embraced them all, one by one, like presents wrapped just for us? To embrace life as it unfolds, trusting in God's ultimate control of the outcome. Wouldn't this serve as a worthy goal?

In this town, this house, this place, I want to cultivate an open, nonjudgmental spirit that takes in both nature and humanity, so I own the growth, the discovery, and the energy of each day. I should print out a sign for my study corner: Let No Aqua Moon Escape Me.

The Shepherd

Our family's short sojourn in the developing country of Senegal, West Africa, in the early eighties rarely comes to mind, but of all our experiences there, I think of the shepherd most often. One other mental image, a gorgeous flowering bush somewhere out in the middle of the desert, tops my recollections. Drowning in culture shock, I kept my eyes on the spot between my husband's shoulder blades as he drove the four of us through incredibly high sand drifts en route to our outpost in the Sahel, the edge of the Sahara Desert.

Our daughter was three, and excited about any trip with Dad and Mom. Our son, less than a year old, transitioned well to travel. But I didn't.

The farther we traveled, the more my stomach rolled. Finally, we had to stop so I could empty the cardboard oatmeal box I'd brought along for such a time as this. Always prone to motion sickness, I found this sand track no better than any other curved, bouncy road.

My spirits, along with my stomach, rose and sank in tandem with the truck that took us to our new home. How could I manage in this wasteland with a nursing baby and a toddler? Back in the United States, I believed if one had faith, obstacles such as the dust allergies our small son now manifested, not to mention my own, could be surmounted.

Just when I felt my willingness for this adventure fading like the signs of civilization in the landscape, something pink appeared a few feet from our moving vehicle. Audacious, enormous pink blossoms smiled at us out of an otherwise pale gray-tan scenario of endless sand. In this unexpected array of gorgeous color, God's kindness blazed. A flowering bush in the desert—I could hang in there.

Needless to say, the reality of daily life bore little resemblance to what we'd imagined back in the States. How could we have come here so ill prepared? That's another story, but today I write about the shepherd because Christmas will arrive in about six weeks, and this particular specimen forever changed my vision of the nativity story.

He stood at our courtyard entrance asking for a pot, but he gave me new eyes. We had survived a couple of weeks of total isolation from all things familiar, enough to know that every morning would bring unannounced visitors.

Villagers had to satisfy their curiosity about our blond children, and they also needed pots. Anything capable of holding liquid qualified, and when we realized the lack of such humble necessities in most of the nearby huts, we emptied every possible container for our new neighbors.

But on this particular day I could find no more vessels to empty. After hearing this news, the old shepherd sat down in a corner to rest. I didn't know how far or how painfully he traveled on his wobbly legs for a pot, and if I could relive that day, I would produce one somehow. Though I didn't grasp it at the time, this man would transform my rather mystical, romantic picture of the shepherds in the Christmas story.

This gnarled herder's wrinkled skin and sun-shrunken face revealed years of futile work etched by drought and famine. Rags covered his bony body in twisted terraces. His feet provided their own brown, calloused shoes, deeply cracked and veined.

Had this man's skin ever known the luxury of soapy water? His scent belied that possibility. No flowing robes for this real shepherd, no relief for weary, lined eyes, no carefully carved staff as he stood in our doorway asking for a pot.

Now he stands somewhere between my mind and my heart, eyes slit like caverns against his homeland's blowing sand. He asks for a pot, but he needs so much more: food, medical care, and to hear the angels' song, as did those shepherds so many years ago on the windswept hills near Bethlehem.

My vision of him still speaks, as do the flowers on that out-of-place bush. The shepherd calls me to attend to the inordinate needs around our hurting world. The bush calms me, enabling me to tend to my own, as well.

Lectio Divina

Pondering Scripture has sustained me ever since I first became aware of the power of this living and active Word of God. I wish Lectio Divina (sacred reading) had come into my life sooner. Stopping to ruminate on the very first word or phrase that strikes me in a passage strengthens and lengthens my meditations.

As a young believer, college group Bible studies required hard work—researching possible applications took much time and attention. The truths gleaned changed my life, but most often those changes were calculated, written down, and shared with the Bible study group so we could "check up" on ourselves. Ours was a serious commitment to a strenuous form of spirituality.

Lectio Divina with its rumination, much like a cow chewing her cud, attracted me. During my introduction, this quiet experience of the Word drew me like light in darkness. A friend and I simply sat with the Scripture, allowing the Holy Spirit to point out the day's truth, which most often appeared in one word or short phrase. Then we considered the word, rolling it around in our minds and hearts.

In this process, what comes to us arrives without our effort—we merely open our hearts and minds to receive. Something about the tranquility of this method corresponds with the serenity I have always sought. Something about the simplicity beckons and nurtures.

The next step of responding has nothing to do with writing out possible applications and figuring out how to complete them to prove one's spirituality. Instead, we dialogue with our Lord about the word or phrase. How does this small portion of holy writ speak to us at this time? What questions do we have? What does the Scripture offer? And most important, will we receive?

Then comes the most wonderful part of all: resting. In our spirits, we recline concerning what we have received. Resting woos me, too, after decades of seeking, searching, striving, and working. Can it be that my part is only to open myself, receive, and rest?

Here's an example: yesterday, Jared, a younger man with bitterness riding just under his smiles, lashed out at a mutual friend. In the aftermath of a messy child-custody case, his stress level careened over the top. His harsh tone hurt.

At lunchtime, my friend called me. She has just begun practicing Lectio Divina, and this morning she read Psalm forty-one. "You won't believe this. Consider this verse from The Message: 'Dignify those who are down on their luck; you'll feel good—that's what God does.'"

She sighed. "I didn't get any further than the first verse today...I didn't need to. I'm resting in *dignify*. Everywhere I turn, I see a new way to dignify Jared. If anyone is 'down on their luck,' it's him. My focus has changed from nursing hurt feelings to how I can give him dignity. Feeling good isn't the most important thing in the world, of course, but I *do* feel good! Last night, I felt sorry for myself and went to bed planning on having a bad day, but it's just the opposite."

Mirror

"Now we see in a glass darkly (or a mirror dimly, as the King James Version puts it)." Paul summarizes his "love chapter," First Corinthians thirteen, with these words. I like the dim mirror image, since I've experienced such a phenomenon. Today we can buy a decent mirror at Wal-Mart for a few dollars and throw out the dim one.

But Grandpa Lawrence used his hazy mirror until the end of his life. He lived alone from the time Grandma died when I was five. I still have a clear mental picture of her springtime funeral, to which I was allowed to wear my new Easter hat.

By the time my teenage interests turned to finding a way to stay in town for ballgames on Friday nights instead of riding the bus to our farm, Grandpa's little house developed into a haven. He barely cooked, so I would make him hamburgers or goulash before the game. It was the seventies, but since my mother's parents always lived on the edge of poverty, this house hadn't been updated except for the installation of a toilet under the stairs of the dank basement.

Finding a mirror to prepare my adolescent appearance for the game proved quite a challenge. Not very adept at coordinating colors or outfits, and hampered by a wretched self-concept, there was no question about it—I had to have a mirror.

Grandpa hung one over the sink, a moldy affair bolted to the wall behind the back door of the kitchen. Coats and work overalls nearly covered the haphazard antique, but here he shaved and washed up. That mirror, now dim even in my memory, supplies a perfect picture of what it means to see in a glass darkly. Full of scratches and smoky areas clouding up right in the spot where you suspected a zit lurked on your chin, the mirror was not much better than nothing. Still, a mirror is a mirror, and I made do.

Years later, I spent some frightening sleepless hours on the couch, swaddled in blankets and searching for comfort during a family trial. One night, I re-read the passage likening our view of things to seeing in a mirror dimly.

My riddled heart, like a bloody stump, needed a mountaintop experience, a full-fledged Christian crusade aimed at healing this raw wound. How could a simple reminder of what it's like to use an old looking glass quiet my racing thoughts and heart?

The answer lies in the Holy Spirit's power and presence. *You don't see the whole picture yet. Caught up in the emotions of this painful time, and so prone to label yourself the culprit, you only realize a vague outline of your journey, while a completely different, clear view of this situation exists. Trust My vision of this picture. Someday you'll see that even your nightmarish wakefulness fits into a meaningful plan.*

As surely as I knew my blankets warmed me, God had spoken. No one else could have comforted me in this way at that particular time. *A mirror dimly*. Yes, dimly. Peace entered my fitful spirit through that one word.

Why do specific struggles plague us? Why does a certain type of person keep showing up in our path, or simply loom there, immovable? Why can't we seem to learn the intended lessons and move on? How is it that we haven't grown stronger, more able to hang on to joy in the midst of troubles?

And why does our judgment always turn inward, as if we bear responsibility for every wrong and hurt in our loved ones' lives? When did the God-sized job of shouldering the weight of human brokenness appear on our personal resume? And even more importantly, will we ever mature out of this recurring cycle victorious and whole? If the lesson—not to blame ourselves, refusing to take on the whole responsibility for the situation—is indeed learnable, why can't we seem to grasp it?

The Almighty's comfort does not necessarily reduce our

question list, but instead brings us to a place of quiet. We sit with the questions and with permission to have few or none of the answers. That's God's role. And often in those times, He whispers a word to our souls. If we receive, if we ruminate, we can rest.

So I can shake my head at all my questions. I can sigh and say, *I don't know. I see in a glass darkly. I'm just a human being and I don't understand everything*. Difficult as it is to contemplate, maybe this particular battle will last the entire length of my earthly sojourn.

I hope not, but that's not for me to know. What I do know matters more than analyzing this conundrum. I am not alone. Someone kind and strong watches over me. That beneficent concept had just begun to tantalize my soul years ago as I stood on tiptoe, stretching to search for an image of my face in Grandpa's sad excuse for a mirror.

The Landing

I turn my back on the dining room floor. We've decided to rip up the layers of linoleum and black goo to expose the original fir planks. But not yet. Not until the bathroom, now gutted and empty, is finished, so I won't think about all the hard work it will take to find that century-plus-old fir.

I open the stair door and glance toward the landing, a pleasant area at the top of the stairs where the eye focuses on a wide, centered window. To the left, a hallway about fifteen feet long leads to four rooms.

Compared to most of the house, this area seems okay for the time being. A new lace curtain over the clean window lets in sparse northern light. Unique spaces—landings—encourage us to pause on our way to somewhere.

My childhood home boasted two landings where the staircases turned. The back one served as a lifesaver, catching me the time I bounced hard, one by one down solid oak steps after a running start as I heard my friend's car horn honking from the yard for our shopping date. The resulting colossal bruise on my backside lasted for weeks and hurt a lot. Without that turn in the stairs, the additional thirteen bounces might have broken something vital.

The turn formed a landing six feet wide. This positive architectural device provided a makeshift closet, for our family had a propensity to store things on the stairs. Since these back stairs connected with the heated kitchen, we created a path that dodged twenty-five-pound sacks of flour, baseball bats, children's toys, and other miscellaneous items randomly tossed on the steps.

Former residents trekked upstairs to relieve themselves. The original builders of the house created two tiny rooms at the top of the stairs. One housed an old black claw-foot bathtub, the other a single toilet. To save money on heating, Dad shut those off and declared the pantry a bathroom. Then Grandpa painted every nook and cranny a lovely shade of green.

The new bathroom's narrow pipes, born to clog, caused Dad to rant about the inordinate amount of hair on our bodies as he put on his plumbing hat to resolve the problem. As the only passageway to get to the basement without going outdoors, the bathroom doubled as a hallway.

The term *relaxing bath* held no meaning in our household. From November through April, the outdoor route boasted snow and ice or mud, and you could count on someone needing to get to the basement double-quick whatever time of day you chose to take a bath. An inevitable bang on the door would sound, and you would have to speed it up.

"Who do you think you are, anyway, the queen of Sheba?"

The other possibility for personal hygiene required standing at the bottom of the basement stairs under a pipe with an attached showerhead, but no curtain. Maybe the tub was not so bad, after all.

If you needed to use the bathroom in the night, the back stairway was the quickest route. Some heat from the kitchen seeped under the door, and the stairwell softened the drastic change in temperature from my room, where I could see my breath. The front stairs' gusty drafts swept over a lovely carved balustrade where you could pretend you were Scarlett O'Hara in summer, but on a winter's night it was long, cold, and dark.

One day at a writers' workshop I attended, we drew a portion of our childhood home from a bird's eye view, the first scene to enter our heads. I drew the back-stair landing from the wooden base at the bottom of the stairs. Why this area, which usually hid in darkness? Especially on the upper stairs, you might as well have been in a cave, since no windows existed. Unless you left the lower door open, no light entered, and leaving the door open made Dad furious.

"Were you born in a barn?" The veins in his forehead formed indignant bulges as his voice rose. So usually the door remained closed, unless Mom searched for something.

So why did that landing come to my mind? Why not the high-ceilinged parlor with the fireplace hearth of forest green stones and a great bronze cover with an engraved cameo? Not that, I guess, because we never used the fireplace, and replaced all this original artwork with pale slender beige bricks that were "in" at the time.

Why not the long hall upstairs, straight out of a cowboy movie, dividing five large bedrooms and ending in the balustrade? Why not the heavy doors, thick golden oak with glass window vents that opened when you pulled on a thin metal rod within arm's reach (if you stood on tiptoe)?

Why not the window seats with ponderous wainscoting extending from their frames about two-thirds of the way to the ceiling? I used to sit in one or the other of them, book in hand, sunlight warming my back. Why not the other landing, built for show, jutting out from the body of the house like a sturdy nose with three long narrow windows embracing the small, oak-lined turn?

And why not the attic, so large the first occupants held roller-skating parties there? Well, maybe I know why not. To get there, a mobile obstacle crunched and slid under your feet as you climbed—piles, literally foot-high mounds, of dead bees that lived in the walls' hollow tiles. These insects claimed the attic as their domain. Until I got used to them, I thought they might be dormant and wake up if I disturbed them, but later learned that live specimens buzzed around only in summer.

I did everything in a dreadful hurry back then, and on into my early forties, when my knee and back started to balk. I can't remember not hurrying up or down the stairs. If headed to the attic, the race became a mad spiral, from the kitchen to the landing to the second floor up onto the attic stairs, around their landing, then up again to the skating rink.

But my sketch—a bird's eye view of the back stairway and the landing—stared up at me as the instructor outlined our next assignment: write about the space. What filled our minds in that area of the house? What memories did it evoke? What emotions?

I've been thinking about those questions ever since. Especially on the way down, this space might have provided an important spot for us to pause and catch our breath before descending into the darkness. What obstacle might have been added to the closet-like cache on the stairs to trip us? What awaited us in the kitchen? We never knew what might hit us when we entered the light.

I'm grateful for landings between experiences, time to rest a bit before plunging into something new, time to process what just happened. As a kid, I didn't waste much time on landings, but habits can change. Maybe in this season of life, I'm called to do more pausing, more waiting.

A window graces our new landing, and the stairs enter into the dining room, the brightest area in the house. My aim is to have fresh flowers on the table as often as possible, making it a perfect spot to ruminate on a Lectio word for the day. I think I'll place a wooden chair in the landing corner, in case anyone wants to sit for a while before they come down the stairs.

If

This morning, a short but powerful word settles over me from the first chapter of Mark's Gospel. A leper came to Jesus in one of the villages as He visited all the meeting places in Galilee. The sick man fell to his knees before the itinerant rabbi and pleaded.

"If you want to, you can cleanse me." What a statement. The man could have begged, "Please, please have mercy on me and cleanse my disease."

Jesus and His disciples were used to people begging for favors, especially for healing. But Jesus must have recognized the man's sincerity and faith.

Mark takes us directly into our Lord's heart. "Deeply moved, Jesus put out his hand, touched him, and said, 'I want to. Be clean.' Then and there the leprosy was gone, his skin smooth and healthy."

How can we enter into this touching scene? We witness the tenderness in the Master's eyes, hear the man's tremulous sigh, smell putrifying open sores, and feel the touch of gentle hands on diseased skin. How long had it been since anyone touched him? The disciples stand transfixed as the leper's sores transform into smooth, healthy skin before their very eyes.

We want to stay here in this holy moment, this heaven-to-earth scenario, to embrace the well of divine compassion that sees and hears and meets a suffering person's needs. How can we even begin to imagine the leper's relief and his dizzy delight? But the story goes on, and my entire day will not be enough time for rumination.

"Jesus dismissed him with strict orders: 'Say nothing to anyone. Take the offering for cleansing that Moses prescribed and present yourself to the priest. This will validate your healing to the people.' But as soon as the man was out of earshot, he told everyone he met what had happened, spreading the news all over town. So Jesus kept to out-of-the-way places, no longer able to move freely in and out of the city. But people found him, and came from all over."

Why this ending? What happened to the healed man after he heard the Lord's admonition? Why didn't he obey his healer? What internal struggle ensued?

Maybe the instructions conflicted with his expectations. Had he seen others leaping for joy after meeting Jesus, shouting their joy to anyone who would listen? Had he visualized his own healing and an exuberant, God-honoring response?

Maybe taking an offering to the priest according to Mosaic law seemed too quiet, too old-fashioned, too mundane. Most likely it contradicted what the man had planned, what he envisioned as an appropriate reaction.

Yet this is what Jesus asked, and He guaranteed this simple act would validate the man's healing to the people. The former leper need not leap and yell and attack the villagers with wild exclamations. In fact, Jesus foresaw that behavior causing problems, so He commanded the man to perform one specific, traditional act.

But the man didn't listen. His own idea of what he ought to do won the internal struggle, but his choice caused a lot of trouble for the One who healed him. I could have ruminated much more on this difficult section.

The more I thought about this passage today, though, the more I returned to one central idea. "If you want to, you can cleanse me."

If. Jesus wanted to, that's clear.

But after the healing, did the Lord's simple instructions go in one ear and out the other because of the leper's own logical ideas fixed in his consciousness? We know the routine—*This is the way a good Christian behaves. This is how God leads people.*

I can relate to that. When God tries to "lead me beside still waters," I often chafe. I think I know better, certain that specific activities are "spiritual," and that I don't have time for still waters. How many times has God had to force me to rest?

"If Jesus wants to, He can..." Not only can He heal lepers, He can help us trust that He really knows what's best. He can calm our anxieties about what people think, even if our guidance seems abnormal. He can change a people-pleasing, insecure soul into someone who knows her own heart and mind and accepts the unique human being He has created.

Beyond our ability to scrutinize the ins and outs of the path set before us, beyond our powers to speculate about consequences and the domino effect, beyond our planned agendas, we need to stop and listen. Deeply moved by our need, Jesus offers, along with healing, instructions designed just for our situation. That's all we need for a miracle.

The Piano

This farm wife graciously offered me a piano. Jenny instructs children, and one of the keys on this instrument kept sticking, plus the irretrievably worn, chipped ivories would cost too much to replace. She decided to buy a new instrument.

"Would you happen to want this old heavy one? If we can't find a home for it, we'll have to tear it apart."

Such a sucker for a deal, of course I drove to her farm for a look. I'd had to leave my piano in our last move—that old friend had already survived an icy cross-country trip in a U-Haul truck a few years ago. I didn't want to risk returning it to the Midwest in a moving van. Here in our new "old" house, I hadn't given any thought to a replacement.

In the midst of rewiring, replacing windows and a furnace, knocking out walls, building headers and painting the kitchen cupboards, a piano didn't even make the bottom of our list. Where would I put one when our belongings already overflowed the house? But the idea that a piano might be out there waiting for deliverance caught at my heart.

In Jenny's living room, I gazed at a work of art. My emotional strings twanged dangerously. I've seen even bigger ones—I could actually see over the top, and noted this positive aspect to report to my husband.

Transporting couldn't be as tough as when my dad and uncle moved a piano a third bigger than this one into a basement, stripping the walls of handrails and quarter round in the process, sweating, swearing, and vowing the piano would never leave its new home. They stuck to their word: I think the piano died with the house.

From top to bottom and side to side, I surveyed her. No longer an "it," this musical possibility took on life as my fingers tingled to touch her. Yes, she needed some work, but the intricate raised designs behind the music stand beckoned. She needed refinished, yet she still would add beauty to a room.

We got into a discussion of Jenny's twenty-eight young students, who faithfully come each week to learn where to place their fingers on the keys. Some continue for years, others drop out during middle school, with so many competing activities. Jenny's refrigerator bears a coloring book picture sent from one of them. A monkey sits at a piano carefully outlined and colored in dark grey. The words *I love you*, printed by young fingers, crawl across the top of the page.

The artwork takes me back. Mrs. Fell, beside me on a wooden bench, patiently goes over finger placement and rhythmic nuances. It's Saturday, and this one happy half hour highlights every week.

Years later, when my piano teacher lay ill in the hospital, I visited her. Her dark brown eyes drew me near. "I knew all about your family." I'm still not sure what she meant.

My recollections include only painstaking attention to musical detail in the miniature lesson room in her small apartment above the Chevy garage. The red-brown brick building faced the courthouse, a dignified structure centered by spacious lawns and tall maples.

What details did Mrs. Fell recall? I'm not sure, but I have an idea. What took place on that piano bench for one dollar and fifty cents per lesson while Mom bought groceries? I'll probably never comprehend the immensity of gift in the exclusive attention of this regular meeting with a caring adult.

In that space and time, words and music entwined like scents on a breeze. The overused word *magical* comes to mind for weekly rendezvous. A practiced, yet nonjudgmental ear adept at listening for dropped notes and lagging tempo, alert to fine distinctions in tone, rhythm, and interpretation of composer's intent. This adult ear bent toward me, her passionately earnest student.

She listened to me as I now learn to listen in Lectio Divina. What one word did she give me that made Saturday afternoons worth the whole long week of practice, worth training my fingers to stretch for the octaves? *Valuable—you are valuable to me.*

Now, decades later, someone offers me an opportunity to save a piano. Will I stand idly by while this worn instrument faces disassembly and ruin? I doubt it very much.

The Piano Room

A lone piano occupied this room, a secondary passageway to the upstairs. That is, in the summertime. It probably never occurred to Mom and Dad to heat the upstairs, doubling or tripling the fuel bill. To insulate the airy, meandering ceilings and walls would have cost even more.

That was why they closed off the piano room, containing the open front staircase, from the other five downstairs rooms. The designer intended this space to welcome guests from the front porch, and hung a distinguished oak front door with a single oval window. Graceful turning stairs and carved banisters, complete with a deep coat closet boasting a mirrored door, occupied more than half the room.

Why did the builders place this room in a farmhouse far from anything even vaguely resembling a metropolitan area? I don't know, but many physical aspects of this building that became our home during the last half of my childhood seemed out of place in our rural neighborhood of enormous barns and small frame houses.

Whatever the reason this room managed to stay in the architect's plans, I gave thanks for its existence. When we moved in, my parents nailed wallboard over thick oak pillars connecting this section of the house to what would become their bedroom. They added a door between the now-hidden pillars and plopped an old hand-me-down piano against the makeshift wall. Exactly what I needed.

For all practical purposes, the piano room connected as much with the upstairs as with the downstairs. From mid-October through May, I had this freezing space totally to myself. Here, several times a day, sometimes for an hour at a time, I practiced my week's pieces for Mrs. Fells on Saturday. As I learned to play, I added other unassigned songs, mostly hymns and old sheet music from my aunts.

In retrospect, that room sparks with emotional intensity. Breath visible in the cold, fingers aching from the point where my coat sleeves stopped, giving myself to the music, I huddled. Terribly out of tune—its ivories riddled into sharp points by my little brother's innocent attempts to play them with his toy metal gun—the piano still made music.

No smoke reached this haven, and no cursing or yelling. Playing loud enough to drown out the television's endless cacophony, I sang the songs with words and created verses for the ones without. Never envisioning myself as a star, I bellowed away with singular intent. If someone had asked my purpose at, say, age fourteen, I would have said something like, "I just love to play."

On Sunday afternoons, my uncle and aunt often came to visit. Uncle Ed was a singer. People still tell how he returned to our local high school to play the tuba in the marching band after his infantry service during World War II, because he missed out on that musical outlet the community offered.

He sang the original version of The Lord's Prayer at his sister's wedding, along with "He," a popular sixties song. The words stayed with me all through my growing-up years, solidified by guilt concerning whopping lies I told, usually to protect myself from getting into trouble. The song speaks of how the Lord can change the world with a touch, how He knows our every lie. How we bring Him such sorrow, but He never hesitates to forgive.

My insistent fear of punishment stole my sleep on many nights. God's wrath, so fire-and-brimstone real, accompanied me to bed, and fear of that fire stalked me. How I hoped the last line of this song would prove true!

Ed would spend a good half-hour or more in the piano room, encouraging me to work harder on sheet music so I could keep up with him the next session. Once in a while, Mom would come in, or request a song. Her favorite was "Wish Me a Rainbow," the theme song from the movie, *This Property Is Condemned.*

And she also liked *Too Young*.

I worked extra hard on those two pieces and sang the words with as much drama as I could muster. Even Dad somehow let it slip that he liked my rendition of "The Ninety and Nine" from the Methodist hymnal.

There were ninety and nine that safely lay
in the shelter of the fold.
But one was out on the hills away,
far off from the gates of gold.
Away on the mountains wild and steep,
away from the tender Shepherd's keep...
And none but the ransomed ever knew
how deep were the mountains crossed,
or how dark was the night that the Lord
went through
'ere He found His sheep that was lost.

I played this hymn often when I knew he sat at the kitchen table two rooms away, enveloped by dusky smoke. Maybe some exchange took place in this indirect process, so in sync with our communication style. Perhaps he received a message from my shaking fingers, cut off from him by thirty feet of floor space, a closed door, and an ocean of fear.

Part Two

Creator God, help me see today what my sin hides from me.
That You are closer than my own thoughts and more faithful than the rising and setting of the sun.
You heal me daily; You lift me up, restore my life, and make me whole.
I give You thanks and bless Your name forever, through Christ my Lord. Amen.
~Adapted from *Daily Texts 2006*

On The Floor

I've spent a lot of time on the floor lately. Cleaning floors is one of those jobs you do when you need to. With a bad knee, I've put off this task more than once. But today, sitting cross-legged on our new kitchen vinyl to remove the paint splatters from my unprofessional strokes, cleaning floors doesn't seem so bad. After a long day of painting kitchen cupboard doors lined up in the garage, any kind of sitting will do. The position brings my paternal Grandmother to mind.

One Saturday evening when I rode my bike the country mile to Grandma's, she glanced up at me from the kitchen floor, dressed in her cotton slip, rag in hand, pail beside her like a faithful pet. Her attention was focused on the multitude of stains and spots covering the farm kitchen's linoleum after a week of heavy traffic, so I doubt she noted my surprised expression.

Cooking for seven—sometimes allowing in a stray lamb that needed to be bottle-fed, having hired men, Grandpa, and my dad traipsing through—it's a wonder the floor could even be bettered by Grandma's ministrations. But she didn't seem frustrated as she carefully scooted about the room, just determined.

What shocked me was her exposed flesh, the skirt of her slip above her kneecaps, her shoulders and arms uncovered. Yet her simple uniform made sense. She had labored for a solid week in that slip and her everyday dress, doing everything from chicken chores to washing clothes to working in the garden.

Before she took her weekly bath, this last travail needed tending, so after a full day of perspiring over next week's baking, why not be as comfortable as possible? The oven had cooled down by this time, and supper dishes, now scrubbed and dried, lined the cupboard shelves. The dog and cats had consumed the leftovers in their outdoor dishes and everyone else had already taken their bath. Finally Grandma's turn had come.

With the week's backbreaking work behind her, she quite possibly enjoyed her time on the floor, and I can relate. After standing all day, relief comes as I lower myself with rag and scraper in hand. The challenge of ridding our new floor of every paint splash seems almost like fun.

Of course, I have a much more comfortable seat to support me than Grandma's. Ancient, cracked linoleum strung over her hard floorboards. Nails most likely ripped through their covering after years of hard wear, catching at her slip as she moved. But she was used to things being tough. When her mother died, she hired out to clean people's homes at eleven years of age.

She had worked ever since, and nothing changed when, clerking in the town's general store, she met Grandpa. His vision entailed every sort of farm work. They lost their first hard-earned farm in the Depression, but gained another one through backbreaking labor.

Grandma's turn for a bath arrived at about eight in the evening on a hot summer's day when I was perhaps twelve years old and she in her sixties. She never put on airs. A physically strong woman who handpicked field corn as a young wife, she had enough spirit left for one more task, even at the end of a grueling week.

How wonderful that shallow bath felt (one must always conserve water and energy), I can only guess. Backpacking in the Rockies with four or five days between taking showers is one thing, but the exertion of climbing steep mountain paths doesn't come close to the kind of heavy lifting Grandma's duties required. Her whole life, she cleaned up other people's messes.

Maybe she complained from time to time, but I don't remember hearing her voice negativity about her lot in life. "If you can't say something good, don't say anything at all," she stated one day when I griped about something or other.

The coolness, the quiet, the chance to rest my feet as my

rag rubs this paint-peppered floor, the sound of cicadas outside taking over for the night—all of these soothe me in some indefinable way. My thoughts of Grandma do, as well. If floor-sitting draws me a bit closer to her indomitable spirit, I'm thankful for this simple job at the end of my day.

The Move

Our family's narrow world broadened considerably when Dad bought land a mile north of Grandma's, but now, no tractor path led our bikes safely to her house. Dad and Mom piled our belongings from the small, two-story frame house into the cranky red pickup. The process took several trips. On the last one, my brother and I got to sit in the back, dusty wind blowing us into a slightly different world.

From now on we would ride our bikes down the main gravel road, fraught with real traffic, to visit Grandma. I would make countless trips down this route during adolescence, at the slightest excuse, either on foot or by bicycle. Grandma's house gave me somewhere to go.

I don't remember when we started calling our grandparents' place Grandma's, but I do know why. My paternal grandpa, not the friendliest to small children, used the razor strap on Dad and the older girls in their family, and he wasn't above spanking us hard if we deviated from his strict English rules. Even accidental misbehavior provoked his hand to flash out and make the culprit wince.

This happened to me just once that I recall, but the experience made me wary around Grandpa. Somehow, I'd managed to hoist myself up on the iron bar above the gate at the yard's entrance and hung there, proudly swinging back and forth. This accomplishment caused jubilation until I had to go "number two."

Only then did I realize I couldn't get down. The bar, about eight feet high, made a formidable drop for a five-year-old.

My discomfort increased by the moment, along with my fear. Grandpa happened along, angry to see me hanging on the bar. As an adult, I understand his concern for my safety. But my cry that I had to go to the bathroom must have irritated him. Instead of helping me down, he whopped me on the bottom, which made matters worse.

That's where the memory stops, and it's probably a good thing. Some memories are better off left "as is." I have some good recollections of Grandpa, too, like his penchant for making popcorn and apples on Sunday nights. He grew the popcorn, and we learned to feed picked popcorn into a hand-turned metal contraption out by the back door. Grinding and churning, it pulled off the golden kernels and belched out the cobs, stripped and ready for the pigs.

Grandpa was nothing if not a hard worker, and he continued into his eighties. He fought the elements and the depression economy to secure land for his family. But the afternoon I met his wrath from such a precarious position contributed to us calling the homestead Grandma's place.

Houses and Memories

We have just one room left. Well, sort of. That doesn't include the upstairs, and we're talking only about painting. A good friend who actually enjoys painting walls and ceilings agreed to help, and both now bear fresh paint, a huge accomplishment. All floors have been covered or cleaned, except the dining room's fir boards, which we plan to sand down and finish next week. Doors still need hanging, trim must be finished, and energy-efficient windows installed.

So many others have lived in these rooms over the years. Were the couples happy? Did the children enjoy security? During the Depression, was there always food on the table at mealtime, or did that generation suffer like my parents' families?

Mom told about eating potatoes three times a day for a three-week stretch. Grandpa was a painter, and very few citizens had money to spare for someone to paint their walls. Finally, he worked on bridges through the Works Progress Administration of the New Deal, but as the family of six children moved from house to house in their small German town, life must have seemed bleak.

We hear tales of a big vegetable garden planted behind our "new" old house, with long, hot days of home canning in late summer and early autumn. People still butchered their own hogs and cattle and filled up the pump house with hams. The women filled fruit cellar shelves with processed meat for the winter. Living in this farming town, most citizens probably had some laying hens in their outbuildings and a cow tied up near the shed.

Recently we attended a fiftieth wedding anniversary celebration replete with family pictures mounted for the occasion, along with a written history of the children's births and other significant milestones. Dancing, dinner, cake, and toasts celebrated half a century of marriage.

What an achievement—fifty years together, beginning with this couple's dating days, including photos of the structures they called home. The sons and daughters who arranged the party shared tales of memories made in each place, and I wondered again about the children born in our house.

What was life like for them? We've seen pictures from the turn of the century, when an open porch graced the north side—the toddlers posing for the photograph now enjoy their golden years. The information available on former occupants supplies hints.

Those children all grew into upstanding, educated citizens entering service professions. They lost loved ones in the Great War, and sacrificed through World War II. When we bought the property, we inherited the study books of one of them, a retired schoolteacher. In the margins hide bits of wisdom. In some, inscriptions from gift-givers cite a kind, faith-filled woman.

Former students in the elementary school across the street tell a different story of their days in her classroom. Now in their sixties, these former students mention her vicious spankings, and recall rolling up their pant legs for her to whip the tender area behind their knees.

Many educators of her era relied on harsh physical punishment to accomplish their goals, but picturing the former mistress of this house in a schoolroom administering severe, painful punishment to little boys stands in stark contrast to her friends' sentiments. No doubt, she had her students' long-term welfare in mind, and her generation could juxtapose severity with kindness more easily than mine. A child disciplined at school would not be coddled at home, but most likely receive more of the same.

Judging from the overall image of this lifelong teacher's life, she approached discipline with a sense of righteous purpose, not rage. It could have been much worse.

Rage

Submerged memories filter into my consciousness in extra-strength form as we become accustomed to this home. As a child, I lived in two houses only a couple of country miles apart. Thinking of the first brings back only a few recollections—few but strong.

There was a little girl
who had a little curl
right in the middle
of her forehead,
and when she was good
she was very, very good.
But when she was bad,
she was horrid.

The schoolmarm who lived here would have found no reason to spank me. The whoppings I racked up at home motivated me to do anything my female elementary schoolteachers asked, and more. True to the jingle, I was very, very good most of the time, but like any child, I did have my moments.

For example, when the heat and boredom of a summer afternoon got the best of me, I'd find a way to make my baby brother and sister cry as I bounced the stroller back to the house over the rough gravel driveway. What urgent call beckoned me? Reading. I read everything I could get my hands on.

The exhausting days had to be long for Mom, with all her outdoor chores, gardening, keeping house, cooking meals, taking lunches to the field for the men during haying time, plus caring for four children. It didn't hurt me to relieve her by watching the little ones, but my moodiness sometimes prevailed.

Mom could swat when we needed reprimanding, but Dad was another story. His anger rose, ubiquitous as cigarette smoke, and he delivered frequent spankings to our naked bottoms with his leather belt.

One vivid memory of the kitchen in our first house centers on deliverance—such a powerful word. On the first sled-snow day of the winter when I was about six or seven, Dad stood out in the corncrib, trying to fix his red pickup. This vehicle ran, mostly, and we liked to ride in it because holes in the floorboards revealed the gravel on the road beneath us as we sped along.

Sunday school taught me that swearing was wrong. Dad's profanity, as much a part of him as toxins to chemical dumps, troubled Mom. We avoided provoking him as much as possible, but my longing for seasonal delights seduced me to the breezy corncrib that afternoon. Our old wooden sled winked at me from the rafters as bitter wind wheezed through the alleyway of the building.

The broken-down truck had a mind of its own, and a little smart-mouthed girl with what Dad called big brown cow-eyes watched him. She stamped her feet on the frozen dirt floor from time to time. The bowels of the vehicle simply would not cooperate. Not a patient person to begin with, every time he looked up, this wide-faced child eyed him. Several times already, she asked if he wouldn't please get the sled down for her.

Finally, the musty old motor gave a sign of life, and the weary farmer made some gesture of relief. The child, arms akimbo, looked up at him with a knowing expression that he detested and asked, "Did the swearing help?"

And then she raced for the house, hell at her heels. Tearing up the back stairs into the drafty kitchen, she flung herself behind her mother, gasping the truth between sobs. Rubber-booted, he splashed into the room with a hand on his belt buckle.

In that one golden, shimmering, magical moment, her

mother spoke, completely out of character, "Now, you know she's right!"

Guilt constricted the girl's tight throat. Fear hung in the air like grayness on ashes. But for some unknown reason, possibly simple fatigue, the slim-nosed farmer eyed his wife and daughter and turned on his heel in disgust.

No sledding joys occurred that day—small price to pay for hope born in a child's heart. A mother's voice could stay icy hands and the crisp, sharp leather of punishment and shame.

That glimmer stayed with me, like the dimly burning wick I would eventually read about in chapter forty-three of Isaiah. Hope had been planted.

Healing

New Testament healings have a hold on me. I can't seem to get enough of imagining the look in the Savior's eyes as He focuses on those stricken with all manner of infirmities. Luke chapter five describes the paraplegic lowered through the roof by his friends. I love their audacity. They're the kind of people most folks admonish. "Shh, can't you see He's *teaching*?"

Maybe somebody did say that, but the friends pushed their way through anyway. Did they think Jesus would leave the area, cheating their friend of his chance? What made them so passionate that they seized that particular moment to reach the Master?

I can't help juxtaposing the healed paraplegic's reaction to Jesus's instructions with that of the leper a few days earlier. Jesus looked straight into his eyes and said, "Get up. Pick up your stretcher and go home." And the man obeyed. He got up, grabbed the stretcher, and walked out in front of everyone.

The man didn't hesitate, even to say thank you. His obedience relayed his gratitude. Perhaps the healed paraplegic knew his obedience would show the mocking religious scholars what was what. After all, he had heard their challenge. "He can't talk that way! That's blasphemy! God and only God can forgive sins."

I put myself in that crowded room lying on a cot, unable to move. The everyday odors of perspiration, cooking oils, and smelly feet fill the air, and the tension of so many human bodies in a small space as people press toward Jesus. My friends lower me right into the midst of the melee, and there's Jesus, looking up at my buddies on the roof, each with a rope in his hands.

I breathe in as deeply as my weak muscles will let me. I search the Rabbi's face as He turns His gaze toward me. His eyes glisten. He fixes them on me, and I hold my breath. It's as if I'm the only person in the room. And then I hear the most remarkable words of my life:

"Son, I forgive your sins."

Something happens inside me, deep down where bone meets bone, where sinew extends to muscle. Energy exudes from the center of my being, and anticipation makes the ends of my fingers tingle. My fingertips tingle? What can this mean?

Then harsh voices whisper in the background something about blasphemy and what God and only God can do. I turn my head a bit, amazed at the movement. But shadows slip over stark faces, lips purse, and rigid jawlines tighten even more. Jesus whirls slowly, searching them out.

His voice, as clear as the stars overhead, rings out. "Why are you so skeptical? Which is simpler to say to the paraplegic, 'I forgive your sins,' or say, 'Get up, take your stretcher, and start walking'? Well, just so it's clear that I'm the Son of Man and authorized to do either, or both..."

Then He looks at me again, and with the buzzing in my ears, a rising tide of the sort of hope I'd never imagined, I almost miss His words. But His strong presence holds me in the moment.

"Get up. Take up your bedroll and go home." His command enters me like a river of determination—His words empower me to do the impossible. I pick up the old stretcher and people swerve back to make way for me. For me! Their expressions astounded, my friends and neighbors, there's my younger brother—yes, they all move back to let me pass.

I feel their stares, glimpse their gaping jaws, their expressions a mélange of shock and wonder. Some reach out to touch my arm. My joints creak and complain, but I keep walking. Someone says, "We've never seen anything like this!" I step over the threshold to a new world.

Back in my everyday world, the Scriptures call to me. "They rubbed their eyes, incredulous—and then praised God, saying, 'We've never seen anything like this!'"

Today's word is *incredulous*—no question about that. And this day, what will I do with this incredulity, this awe at what Jesus can do? First of all, I can praise.

Oh Lord of all, may my flighty, impetuous existence appropriate and extend Your passion for the healing You can bring to me and through me. And may I never lose this star-struck incredulity that You care enough to be involved in whatever touches my life.

Tenacity

A long time ago in a college setting, I worked with a student enrolled in a basic writing course for the third time. The year before, he had attempted a one hundred level class but, frustrated and discouraged, had now been sent back to the development course. Imagine trying to write essays in a language you barely understand and some of whose sounds you don't even hear.

My heart went out to him, and his situation raised my ire. The college boasted a swimming pool and up-to-date exercise machines. Why couldn't they hire an ESL tutor for this man? On top of that, every staff member used his last name as his first. After *three* courses for which this institution gladly took his hard-earned money, they still didn't know his name?

Sorry, I got off on a tangent there. But a Robert Frost quote gripped me today. "Our very life depends on everything's Recurring till we answer from within."

Recurring is a powerful, potentially unpleasant word. None of us wishes to repeat lessons we've already studied, but progress requires that we do. In the case of my former student, until English fundamentals formed *inside him*, he had little hope of writing a college essay. Spiritual progress is no exception to this rule.

We read how time and again Jesus revealed Himself to the impetuous Peter. We follow his story and keep expecting him to "get it," but the process isn't quick or easy.

The brash fisherman and other disciples needed lesson after lesson, example upon example. So many times Peter stumbled, yet God incarnate didn't give up. At the end, with His time on earth running out, Jesus told Peter he would face enemies and hard times in the future. And He gave him a huge encouragement—he prayed for Peter's faith not to fail. Whatever else Peter remembered as the years passed, surely he clung to that promise. A person's faith could fail, but that wouldn't stop the Lord's support.

Some people couldn't handle the truth, but Jesus didn't apologize for His words or castigate Himself for failure when some didn't believe. He accepted reality: light entered the darkness, but they resisted it. Then they destroyed it...or so they thought.

After "The End," Peter's impetuous nature didn't hinder the risen Jesus from giving him marching orders, along with supernatural gifts. And Peter's personality didn't prevent Jesus from prophesying his gruesome death. The Lord kept on telling Peter the truth, always aiming for clarity.

Peter's life depended on recurrence. So do ours. So does the student's I mentioned, although I did apologize to him for the system's incompetence.

When our lives seem like one endless, repetitive cycle—when it seems we aren't learning anything—we do well to consider the necessity of recurrence. Our dining room floor, hidden under layers of black goo, linoleum, and dusty, faded carpet (green, of course), teach me about recurrence.

I'm hard at this project now. Only intense scrubbing and scraping unearth these boards' golden beauty. Each day I say to myself, "One more good, long day and this should be finished." Of course it isn't, and I say the same thing the next day with more fervent desire. But recurrence does produce change, albeit slowly.

In the same way, our soul-life requires recurrence. What's interesting is how recurrence can drive negative lessons so deep into us that we see little hope for transformation, even after the passage of much time. A father cannot slash his belt on his children's backsides forever, because those children grow into adults. But they often take the punishment inside.

They might become so hard on themselves, so full of self-loathing, that by comparison, the childhood pain seems like nothing. In that case, growth will require consistent recurrence of love messages. Self-acceptance and resting in unconditional love may seem an impossible goal.

But it's all right. The One who died for people like Peter—people like me—has infinite patience and all the time in the world. He knows all about the necessity of recurrence and does not become weary in well doing.

Riding Bikes

Riding a bike with the sun on your back—it doesn't get much better. A self-made breeze cools the lucky rider, and objects flit by, giving a sense of getting away from whatever they need to escape. For me, the decades have not altered this effect. Something about increasing our speed frees us and quiets our minds. When I've had to temporarily give up bike riding, getting back on always launches a natural high.

When my husband and I returned from a developing country twenty-some years ago, one of my first pleasures was riding a borrowed bicycle. The homemade contraption boasted a child's seat hooked to the front handlebars and another attached to the back. Riding around town with my precious double cargo administered the best possible medicine during that disturbing time of disappointed dreams.

Cycle inventors rank high on my list of innovators, right up there with the Romans, who gave us hot showers. The older I get, the more a twenty-minute pedal around town revives me.

On an island where I went for our first grandchild's birth a few years ago, we tried to find a bike for me to ride during my six-week stay. A far more daunting task than we imagined, bicycle shops offered nothing below $250, and second-hand stores displayed pieces of genuine rusted-out junk for over $100.

New replicas of what we sought—an old Schwinn that had seen better days but still worked—sold for about four hundred dollars. We finally purchased a large child's bike, which served the purpose, but I thought it strange how few bikers I met on the island. Back in the Midwest, students still ride their bikes to school and around town afterward. Quite a few baby-boomers pedal their way to work or the grocery store, and I happily join them. But lately, my main goal in riding is to escape from painting, sanding, or staining.

Our eighty-year-old neighbor flies by through the alley once in a while, looking young and agile. Watching him, I feel some hope about aging. He looks so carefree. I love walking, but for me, it goes with thinking, while the rhythm of biking de-clutters my brain.

A few days ago, coming up a slight hill down the street from our house, the chain flew off my bike, a garage sale three-speed. The broken chain precipitated my search for an old-fashioned bike without speeds. I've never figured out how to use the speeds, anyway. A man in town loves bicycles, and we chatted over a dark red, no-speed bicycle to which he was attaching a handlebar basket.

This connoisseur has collected over two hundred models. He purchased the old town hall of a teeny town near here for storage. Why does he do this? He likes to. His full-time job involves motorized vehicles, but when he comes home, he works on bikes. The hobby has overtaken his garage and basement as well as a building he bought for storage. What does he do with them? Every once in a while he sets up a tour, he says.

As I rode off toward home on my new-to-me bike, he called, "You look good on that one."

There ought always to be bikes to ride. It's the closest someone like me will ever come to the wild liberty of Olympic skiers or professional skateboarders. I intend to continue toddling along on my old Schwinn until the next life, when "I'll fly away."

One More Bike Chapter

"Oh that I had wings like a dove, for then would I fly away, and be at rest."
~ Psalm 55:6 (KJV)

Today, my husband and I resorted to the ice scraper from the garage. Yes, after testing several solvents, it turns out that what works is plain old tap water. We pour it on a patch of the black underlayment that hides what we believe will be a gorgeous fir/oak floor. (Two wood experts disagree on which one, but we'll take whatever comes.) And two family members from the greatest generation stare at us and ask a pointed question. "Haven't you heard of Pergo?"

Yes, we have, but we want the real thing. So we wet down an area, let it soak for a few minutes, and then attack it with the ice scraper. Seriously. I sit down to do it because my knee is starting to balk. And from time to time, I turn to my childhood escape: bike riding. Even ten minutes away from this tedious task does wonders.

Kids in our rural neighborhood rode bikes for joy, but subconsciously, riding may have provided a means of escape. Wisps of emotional information from our childhood come to us in snitches and snatches, and little by little, God's Spirit weaves them into our understanding.

In those days, I had other survival tools I didn't realize as such, like writing and reading. Try denial, controlling, blaming, and minimizing. Several years ago, for the Oregon state summer writing project, participants wrote our writing autobiographies, and during the process, several of these coping mechanisms popped up. I titled my story "Writing Against the Darkness."

Reading this treatise aloud to the other participants exposed the raggedness of our souls—several of us added tears to our offerings. Here I was, an adult woman with such a shaky voice that one of the professors offered to read for me. I thanked her but continued. I needed to do this.

> *Mom and I sat at the kitchen table as she taught me to put pencil to paper, crafting my first word...my name. Bless her! To this day, pencils remain my favorite writing tool, and writing serves as a monumental healing agent. The act of expressing emotions on paper became, like riding bikes, a way of processing life. Even if you could not escape physically, you could go somewhere else for a while.*
>
> *I must have been about four years old that landmark day, in a realm without bright crayons, coloring books, Sesame Street characters, classical music (or any music at all), authors discussed over dinner, or any highfalutin ideas of academic pursuits. Life was lean and spare in this midwestern farmhouse. We rarely called long-distance and wasted nothing on a daily newspaper, a way of life typical of most families in our rural community.*
>
> *No wonder the two-mile trip into town for Sunday school seemed such an adventure. There, once a week, we heard stories complete with pictures, papers scripted with written meaning to hold in our hands and tote home as treasures. Someone played the piano, gentle women smiled at us and taught us to sing, men greeted one another without profanity, and the low wooden tables, smooth to the touch, smelled*

shiny clean.

Teachers read to us, asked us questions, and listened when we answered. Above all, they entrusted us with crayons, pencils, and pens. Memories of that cool cinder-block church basement exude acceptance and hope.

When the immense possibilities of the public school system presented themselves, I felt instantly at home. My kindergarten teacher, amazed at how much time I spent cleaning the restroom sink with real Comet, shared her observation with Mom during conferences. I was a good reader, so she didn't mind.

Clearly this place of creativity, light, and learning delighted one hungry little girl. By the end of elementary school, consuming books developed into a passion, and writing down my thoughts came a close second. Long walks, playing the piano, and bicycle rides rewarded caring for younger siblings, housecleaning, fieldwork, lawn mowing, and the endless cooking and baking required on the farm.

I enjoyed most of the work, especially mowing our huge lawn, which provided another chance to walk and the satisfaction of clean-cut corners when I finished. Activities like this became inspiration for writings, carefully hidden away. When the night terrors came, I wrote. When a teacher said, "Write an essay," I reveled.

Once, a high school English instructor penned, "Your writing shows real talent," at the top of an assignment. After class, I asked if he really meant what he'd written. He said he did, and I longed for his words to be true.

When I heard about Paul Engel's writing courses at the University of Iowa, I longed desperately to attend, but the darkness wouldn't let me. My words poured out, instead, on family vacations in the backseat of our smoke-infested Ford containing five children, two frazzled parents, dense smoke, and no air-conditioning, jars of baby food gurgling in a porcelain heater plugged into the cigarette lighter. But those words remained sequestered.

Mom tried to get a peek, but these writings revealed the inner me I felt the need to hide. If she were to read my actual thoughts, what would be left of me? My writing seemed important, but I had no idea that it equaled survival.

Poetry continued to spurt sporadically, always on Emily Dickinson themes. A college creative writing class challenged me. After graduation, I taught special education and began to come out of my stunted adolescence, drawn into the light by a community of caring Christians.

Lance and I married a few years later, and he completed his seminary training. With a nursing infant and a toddler in tow, we departed for a proposed career in the mission field. A line from a book sent in a care package motivated me to submit a poem for publication. The quote went something like, "If you have a gift you don't use, you stand to lose it."

Fear motivated me to dig through my writing cache. I sent one poem to this "safe" person, a writer herself, asking if she thought it might qualify for publication. A magazine editor purchased the brief manuscript when she submitted it. Finally, I began to believe that this part of me sent out into the world was acceptable, even desirable. Of course, this experience motivated more writing.

A year and a half later, back in the United States, reverse culture shock compelled me to write a short book on the abortion issue. We returned from a country where fifty percent of the children died before age five, to a land where women protested for their rights. To my amazement, a small company bought my manuscript for current issues classes and asked me to produce another on suicide.

A few more attempts, some successful, at having poetry published over the next decade, entitled me to a "brag file" of rejection slips, but also the joy of publication. My writing journey became a try-for-a-while, be rejected, and quit process.

But in the early nineties, a totally unforeseen situation involving child sexual abuse emerged in my extended family. The shock threw me into writing with a savage intensity. This time I knew writing pertained to survival. I also rode my bike fanatically during that time.

Processing a revelation concerning abuse requires immense introspection and therapeutic effort. The powerful trauma threatens everything essential. My gut-level response, revulsion coupled with sheer terror, inflamed my days and nights with anxiety. Our extended family split between support for the children and their mother, Ellen, and denial that enabled the perpetrator.

When it was over—as much as this shattering can ever be over—I had filled a ream of paper with verses describing the anguish of discovery coupled with the exquisite comfort God supplied. The writings focused on grief and loss, not abuse. My life wrapped around those words poured out to comfort and encourage hurting family members.

I'm writing vicariously, I thought. The death and grief themes concern Ellen's work with the dying. And Ellen did find encouragement in my writings, which eventually became sympathy cards for people in loss and transition. As the state president of her organization, she used them for a fundraiser later that year, with positive response.

"People exhibit their products at our conventions. You could do that next year." I told her I had no business sense, the left side of my brain lay undeveloped, I had a money neurosis and simply could not do what she suggested. But her confidence caught at my spirit as positive responses to the cards continued. Against my better judgment, I shakily launched a home-based card line the next spring.

To shorten a long story, that experience led to traveling the nation. At a deeper level, the world of shame in which I'd lived for half a lifetime transformed into a place of healing. A book on suicide found its way on to paper, unbidden, and finally I came to process this outpouring as baggage from the past. Invitations to facilitate grief workshops led to speaking, with the theme of teaching people to journal through grief.

For two years I dug old manuscripts out of files and edited them. I learned not to take the rejection slips so personally—editors weren't rejecting my writing, my submission simply didn't fit their agenda at the time. Out there in the wide world, there was still a place and a need for my voice.

Most often, a labor of love is necessary for our denouement. Like scraping off glued black gunk to reveal antique floorboards in our dining room, the work grinds at our spirits. But time will reveal treasures that lurk in veiled places as someone comes along who cares enough to coax us out of hiding. The pain inherent in exposure bears worthy fruit in the end, and taking a wee bike ride now and then can provide just the break we need.

Old Doors

Yesterday carpenters performed major surgery on the front wall of our house, buzz sawing through sturdy timbers from 1875. As they added more windows in the living room, the workers discovered a door hidden behind the flimsy, exposed insulation held by boards placed there one hundred thirty years ago—only ten years after the Civil War ended.

Finding the door increased the time and stress of the carpenters' task, but they unearthed a treasure. Touching those rough-hewn timbers with my fingers seemed necessary and right. Other rooms shuddered with the deep grinding of electrical power as saws tore into the building's very beginnings, but what they sawed through shouted history.

Neighbors came to take pictures and watch the header fall into place to prevent eventual sagging. (If you've never lived in a small town where everyone knows everyone, you'll wonder why. If you have or do live in such a village, you will understand. I'm kind of surprised our newspaper didn't run a front-page feature.)

People once walked through this opening to worship, since our house served as the Lutheran parsonage before the church was built. Six or seven families have inhabited the space since that time, babies crying their way into the world, children running and playing tag, elderly women rocking away long winter days.

Did volunteers work together with the family to complete this house in an old-fashioned "house-raising"? Did the congregation bear the cost? With very few other settlers here, where did the pastor's family live while their house took shape?

It's no light thing to saw through layers of time. I called our neighbor two doors down, a member of the church for which our house served as a parsonage. She came with her camera, and we also invited Grace, who was birthed in this house. Her sight limited, she reached with trembling fingers toward the original beams. Watching her animated face, I knew others shared my sense that present and past met here.

Not long ago, a student in one of my classes bought a church building in a nearby town to transform into a home for his young family. Considering its location in a residential part of the town, new siding, windows, and a firm foundation, this couple congratulate themselves on making quite a buy. Soon, wild little boys and girls will tumble through the rooms, living life. I'm happy for them.

On a detour from class the other night to drive by their new home, I whispered to no one in particular. "I don't know if I could live there." All the decades of prayers uttered under that roof, all the gut-wrenching funerals, all the people baring their souls to God in that silent sanctuary. I know it's just a structure, but it seems like more than concrete and beams, stairways, floorboards, and walls.

Our house, used only temporarily as a place of worship until the actual church was completed, had no "sanctuary" as such, but my student's new home served a congregation until recently. The air must still be filled with mourners' cries and seekers' longings. Many sanctuaries have absorbed my own joys and sorrows.

Oh, I know that the Almighty dwells in flesh, not buildings. No doubt, it's all a matter of perspective. My student would say, "It's only wood, brick and plaster, windows, doors, ceilings and floors, a basement and a roof. When we've completed our work, this home will be just like any other."

He's probably right, and the book of Revelation tells us that in the new heavens and earth, no temples will be needed. God will be our temple there, and after all, doesn't He come to live within us? Why should anyone have qualms about living in "sacred space"? The heavens and the earth belong to our Creator; isn't every space sacred?

Some pioneers felt the same, undeterred by Native American

burial grounds or other holy places. For tribes who had honored their sacred grounds for centuries, their audacity caused great disturbance and resentment.

Next to our computer lies an invitation to a program celebrating Henry Melchior Muhlenberg, missionary to America in 1787, ninety-three years before our house existed. This missionary found relatively few sacred spaces constructed by pioneers, although he probably trod on some holy to Native Americans.

The idea of honoring holy places takes us back to Abraham, and Proverbs 23:10 instructs us to honor ancient boundaries. A woman I know spends time living among Native American peoples and studies their history, including our nation's tragic, pathetic treatment of the tribes and their holy places. Often, Christendom wandered far from its moorings in the compassionate Christ in relation to these peoples. I wonder if Muhlenberg honored tribal heritage and lands?

Nearly another century had passed after his journey to the new world before German immigrants in our community committed their time, effort, and money to build their parsonage-church in our fledgling town. What filled their minds? An interesting side note reminds me that nearly twenty years earlier, Norwegians completed their sanctuary just a few blocks away.

Obviously, these believers' very specific faith motivated them. They would have a pastor of their own now, one who spoke their mother tongue. They would have a church. Meeting in our living room marked one significant stepping stone on the way to their ultimate goal.

The carpenters will cover these old boards up again, presumably forever. But the morning sunlight shone on the past for a while, reflecting something from history worth considering. Our house has survived a significant upheaval. Something was lost in the process. We can call it sameness, or the status quo. But in its place, two new windows will let in twice the light.

All Saints Sunday

Last week, a neighbor graciously offered to hang a heavy mirror above a low shelf. After creating an enormous hole in our new plaster to hold a toggle bolt, he discovered there was no stud at the spot he drilled. The toggle bolt wiggled around, meagerly suspending what needed much stronger support. We left things "as is" at the time, but when he went home, we shoved the entire bolt through the hole, back into the recesses of the wall where it now lies undisturbed—except for by the occasional mouse or bat.

How many other bolts and nails, screws and nuts, plus who knows what else, lurk behind plaster in this house? Watching that piece of steel disappear reignited my interest in "things hidden." Today, All Saints Sunday, the season of bringing the past to light, brings to mind those who've gone before. What "emotional toggle bolts" do we push through dark holes in hopes they will disappear forever, only to have them reappear in some form or other in the future?

This morning's service began with a prayer of thanks for the saints who have colored our lives. First on the list were the apostles, of course, and then came others. The one on the list preceding "mothers who dandled us on their knees" was the last I could say out loud, since this word picture of Mom caring for me as an infant sparked tears, pushed my strongest guilt button, and rendered me incapable of speech.

Will I ever stop feeling guilty about our relationship? Our history includes such bad vibrations. So many well-intended visits that ended in arguments, so vast a sense of detachment, so little heart-sharing.

For a person who values story, there seemed to be no capacity in me for drama when we were together. Pretending escaped me. This was my mother; I wanted us to be real. Yet I could not accept her reality, laced with denial, any more than she could mine.

Now, years have passed since she died. That last year, I called every week, but long silences filled most of the airtime. Still, she comes to me on days like this, in a prayer on All Saints Sunday.

No one would ever imagine a toggle bolt rests in the bones of our dining room behind the mirror, but I know. In the same way, no one surmised the heavy fog of guilt that gripped my consciousness as the service proceeded. No, this was my work, and this type of visit happens often enough that I've learned to sit with it, thinking, not thinking, crying, waiting.

"For all the saints," we sing, "who from their labors rest... we feebly struggle, they in glory shine." Maybe comfort lies in this concept. Mom struggled so. Life could not have been easy with five children to care for, unspoken, unfulfilled dreams, and only the barest smidgeon of self-esteem.

Yet I honestly think she did the best she could. Mom initiated any glimmer of hope in our sparse world. In an atmosphere of negativity, grudge holding, punishment, and condemnation, she beaconed the darkness.

I remember one day when I heard, in horror, the same curse words Dad constantly used spout from her mouth. Maybe the hopelessness of the daily grind sent her over the edge. I remember facing the east wall of the living room, listening to her younger sister calm her.

Mom—the one who saw to it that we made it to Sunday school most weeks, who once in a great while mustered the courage to stand up to Dad when he threatened us with another beating—Mom, losing it? Aunt Sue shooed us away, saying everything was all right, but my little person stared, terrified.

I'll always wonder what troubled her so that day. What happened to cause her emotional overload? Who knows? Children always jump to the conclusion that they've caused the problem. I don't know if I did or not. But the words *feebly struggling* apply, and struggling doesn't necessarily imply failure.

Struggling means not giving in or not giving up. Most of the time, Mom managed to keep things in our household from blowing out of control, but all of us have our seasons of frailty and weakness. Age can lead us into that feeble struggle to which the songwriter alludes.

Nowadays, with helpful literature and support groups, a mom might leave for her own sanity. But one can give up while remaining physically in place. Resignation can induce a coma-like detachment. However it was for our mother, she still communicated love and kindness. No grandmother ever loved her grandchildren more.

I do so hope she shines now in glory. She had a great smile and loved to sing—hopefully she does a lot of both.

My turn has come to feebly struggle, not with the heavy task of rearing five children on a stark farm in a tyrant's shadow, but in dealing with the aftermath.

Part Three

Benediction for Women

May the God of Esther cause you to shine like the stars as you stand against evil.

May the God of Sarah give you grace in living with your imperfect Abrahams.

May the God of Mary, Jesus's mother, give you a heart of obedience.

May the God of Mary Magdalene give you a calming peace.

And may the God of YOU empower you on your journey through this life.

Friendship

Older women's stories give us hope. Grace, whom I met years ago in a creative writing class, has re-entered my life. Who could have known we would buy the house in which she was born? Her stories, honest, but full of cheer and positivity, remain with me after our visits.

She tells, for example, about her move as a young bride to a run-down farm on beautiful creek land a few miles from a small town. At first, entranced by the lovely area, she could only see the situation through romantic eyes. It was 1947, and her husband of seven months returned from war two years earlier.

A wildness ran in this man's veins, a spirit of adventure, somewhat tamed after being taken prisoner at the Battle of the Bulge. He nearly starved to death toward the end of the war. Emaciated, he returned to Schick Shadel Hospital in southern Iowa to recuperate.

Grace knew she wanted to attend Iowa State University to become a home economics teacher from a young age. But she had no money. An aunt loaned her a hundred dollars, and she worked odd jobs around town for two years to save enough to attend Iowa State Teachers College. Like her older sister, Grace attained the summer country school teaching certificate.

She taught for several years and saved five hundred dollars for one semester at Iowa State. Then she worked her way to graduating with a home economics degree in 1941 and taught in western Iowa.

During World War II, she accepted a position in Cedar Rapids. In 1946, Grace accompanied some business people who spent weekends helping out with crafts and other activities for the returned POWs occupying the hospital rooms. Her brother's childhood friend Allan had recently arrived at the hospital, so

Grace agreed to try to find him, since his family had not yet been able to see him. In fact, from December 17, 1944 until April of 1945, they didn't know whether he was alive or not.

Eight years her senior, this fellow had stopped by their house several times during her brother's high school years, but Grace's dim recollections stemmed only from the brief periods as Allan waited for her brother to go fishing. An elementary school student at the time, would she even recognize this soldier if she saw him?

Since workers could not enter patient wards, Allan would have to come out into the public areas for her to greet him. Working in the craft room one Saturday, Grace happened to look up as a man who seemed familiar strode by on his way to the cafeteria. By this time she was thirty-one years old and dating the superintendent of another school.

Not the type to seek a man simply for the sake of having one, she had already introduced her administrator friend to her parents. She figures they would probably have married someday if Allan hadn't shown up. Realizing this must indeed be her brother's old friend, she jumped up and ran after him. He answered to the name Allan, and seemed pleased to see her. She gave him greetings from his hometown, and he invited her for a cup of coffee—their first date.

"As soon as we met, I knew he was the one for me." She smiles at her admission. The two became engaged at Christmas, and the next summer, they married in the German Lutheran church down the street from her childhood home—our house. Allan's proclivity to wander produced no savings for the future, but Grace speaks only of his courage to leave home and hearth as a young man.

After high school, he struck out for Montana to farm with a friend, but after six years, went bankrupt. His friend married and stayed out West, but Allan returned home and found a job as a cream truck driver until his younger brother Joseph received his draft notice.

After their mother died in their youth, Allan always took care of his little brother. When the draft notice arrived, still hungry for adventure, Allan volunteered to take Joe's place in the Army. Much better suited for the task than his quiet, gentle younger brother, he relished his military adventure.

After the war, when Allan and Grace moved to the farm, Joe went right along. This kind man became a big help around the house and a wonderful uncle to Grace and Allan's children. It wasn't uncommon for a brother to help out on a farm in those days, or to live with his brother's family, and Grace, a town girl until her marriage, soon realized she could use every bit of available assistance.

Carrying water was the worst, especially in the incessant mud of spring and autumn. The homestead, unoccupied for twenty years, boasted no modern improvements and a massive amount of work. Before they moved in, Allan brought in electricity but said plumbing would have to wait.

Five years later, Grace still waited for indoor plumbing when her friend, a dress design instructor, came to visit. They met during college, and Marcia had grown into a perfectly coifed, lovely woman. She fell in love with the farm and went out of her way to pay individual attention to Grace's two young children, to Grace, and to Allan.

"She saved my marriage. She saved my life." This high praise for a friend evokes a furrowed brow and a shake of Grace's head.

Marcia's visit "was like a fresh breeze blowing over my life." The light in Grace's eyes backs up her words. When she complained about her lot during Marcia's visit, her college friend listened, and then threw back her head with a strong laugh.

"You have a beautiful life!" she said. Grace, stunned and speechless, stared at her.

"Easy for her to say," I fume, but Grace refuses to agree.

"Marcia gave me exactly what I needed. She said, 'You must write down all that happens out here. Describe your days on the farm with your husband, your two sweet children, and Uncle Joe. Write it all down, the endless water pails to carry, the scrubbing and washing, the baking and cooking. Write it all down.'"

I still want to place a little blame on this pampered urbanite who could afford to get her hair fixed at the beauty shop in 1952 when Grace, confined to the farm for days on end, could afford no such luxury. But Grace sees cups half full and makes only positive comments about her lifelong friend.

"She saved my life," she repeats. "I started writing a little book—*Life on the Farm with Allan.*"

Those stories reveal the Allan-centeredness of her existence. Grace acknowledges this, but that's the way most marriages functioned during her generation.

"And I loved him," she stalwartly declares. She leans toward me and pats my arm to enforce her point.

"He never lost his adventurous spirit. Once the team got away from him and made a mad dash down the long driveway into the yard. They went around four times, with the wagon swaying crazily and Allan yelling, 'Whoa! Whoa!' at the top of his lungs.

"Finally, he drove them straight into the side of the corncrib, where they had no choice but to stop dead still. One other time, Joe and Allan were coming in from the field with a full load of oats, because a rainstorm bore down on the farm. Everyone else came in to dry off, but I noticed Allan wasn't in the house.

"When I looked outside, he lay spread-eagle on the top of the wagon, rain driving down on every inch of his body. He held down a canvas to protect the oats from the rain, and stayed there through the entire storm."

She admires him still. "I knew the farm was something he wanted," she states without regret, "and so I wanted it too. Oh, I still complained, especially to Marcia, but she could see the love, which is all that mattered."

Ah—a statement to pause and ponder. If Grace could've chosen a word for this period in her life, what would it be?

Finally, after twelve years of marriage, Allan broke down at Grace's insistence and hired a plumber to lay pipe for running water. Until then, every time she mentioned this need, he ignored her request. Once, he brought in a pail of water from the pump, plopped it down, picked up a dipper, let the water run out, and said, "There. If it's running water you want, here it is."

My questions rise dumbfounded, "But Grace. By nineteen fifty-five, almost no one went without running water. Why do you think Allan persisted in being so stubborn about this?"

She gets a faraway look in her eyes. "Well, there was so much to do. All the fences were broken down. It took years to get them up completely so the cattle wouldn't run into the road, so the pigs wouldn't come and root out the garden I'd just planted. The work was endless."

I can't resist. "But wouldn't the work have been a whole lot easier if you hadn't had to carry all the water?"

She gives a little grin. Obviously, she gave this up to her Father long, long ago. Everything revolved around Allan. And Marcia came for a full week every summer, bringing gifts, excitement, and encouragement. Marcia reminded her of the wonderful life she had, played games with the children, and gave Grace hope.

Seeing the cup half full, she literally twinkles as she hands me a notebook of her stories entitled, *Life on the Farm with Allan*.

Attached to the front page, a photograph of Marcia—with her glowing face, perfect hair, and stylish clothing—smiles at the reader. The title ought to read, *The Tenacity of a Woman* or *The Power of a Friend*.

Lights in the Windows

"I just had to call and say how much I like looking down the street now." Our neighbor appreciates the single candles in each of our living room windows. "Your house is smiling. It stood empty for so long, but now it radiates warmth and love."

I'd like to say my heart radiated like that, in a continuous show of courage and cheer. That's a goal. Candles in the window may belie coldness within walls.

But when I hear Grace's stories, I'm certain the light coming from her home out in the country was real. Then I think, *Maybe her battles with depression and isolation are not so different from mine.* Tales of her mother's life give me food for thought as I pour yet another coat of goo remover on an area of the dining room floor. Her mother, Virginia, lived out her days in this very house. She paced this very floor and stared out these very windows.

Virginia

The isolation of her situation constricted Grace's life. Her husband and his brother could happily work sunrise to sunset, with only a break on Sundays for the trip to church. The heavy duties of cooking, cleaning, gardening, preserving food, sewing clothing, and childcare became Grace's burden, with no outlet for her intellect and no cultural input.

Decades earlier, she had witnessed firsthand what a lifestyle like this could do to a woman—she remembered her mother's three nervous breakdowns. Virginia, one of seven children born in the early twentieth century to a busy and important pastor in this small town, had at times in her adult life ceased functioning, confined to bed for weeks, unable to open her eyes. She would stay at home for six months, Grace recollects, never venturing to the stores one block away, never leaving the yard.

"What exactly do you mean by a 'nervous breakdown'?" I had often wondered what the label meant in practical terms.

"With seven of us, all the responsibilities of food preparation, making clothes, supporting our carpenter father, and organizing the family, Mother found no time for her love of learning and music. She had no time to read, no time for herself as a woman apart from the round of work that made up her life. The doctor told me in later years that she was totally exhausted, mentally, physically, and emotionally."

Grace sees her mother sitting close to the radio in a straight-backed chair along the west wall of the dining room on Saturday afternoons at a certain time, cupping her ear to the speaker of the family's first radio, immersed in the metropolitan opera. The regular household commotion continued around her while she escaped to this private, peaceful realm.

I see Mom with her Sunday newspaper, and Susanna Wesley

in a household teeming with children, taking refuge under her own apron. Somehow, these women stayed in the fray, although they feebly struggled at times. Virginia, worn out in every way, without fleeing the premises, found a way to remove herself.

Aware of all this, very soon after the beginning of Grace and Allan's life on the farm, Grace told Allan that she could do this hard work, but he would have to take her away from it all every once in a while. Her mother's image hovered before her, as it lingers before me hours after our latest chat. Virginia, a strong woman, ghostly for three six-month periods of her life, unable to even wander through the rooms of her own home.

This house has gained several since the early 1900s. Someone moved the stairway so that the west wall of the dining room no longer sits precisely where Grace recalls. However, the room itself is still in the same place, and the fir and pine planks we labor to uncover are the same ones on which Virginia's feet rested as her heart swelled with the musical strains she loved.

It's impossible not to be caught up in the drama of this woman's life. Three nervous breakdowns, three times when darkness closed in, when the will to struggle fizzled in defeat. Her story perplexes, engages, and has been passed down for women who tread the ragged edges of their dreams.

Virginia poises in her chair, ear to faraway rhythms, regardless of the chaos around her. She sits there in my mind and heart, so real I can almost envision her against the afternoon sun's rays. She is my sister, your sister.

Then one morning, she stays in bed, unable to face another day, another moment. Today, help is available when one's spirit becomes so utterly devastated, but Virginia had to bear her inner meltdown here in this house, in the presence of her husband and seven raucous children. And, I might add, in a community with little or no understanding of her quandary.

Her older daughters took on most of the housework and childcare, and Grace describes her father as a caring, gentle man whose wife's three long absences baffled and bewildered him. Anyone with relatives or friends battling emotional or mental challenges can relate.

"He was very good with the children," Grace says. "He would make up games with a dishpan and a handful of peanuts. My memories are of laughter." For her, no matter what, the glass remains half full.

Grace's father carried brandy-laced eggnog into the bedroom, a concoction suggested by their doctor to woo her back from the border of tomorrow. We see this weary husband and father attempt to hold together his work, his family, his wife, his life.

What did the community think when such a vigorous woman dropped out of the known world for six months at a time? Did the neighbor women, the women of the church, bring in meals? Or did they hold themselves apart, this mental and emotional "dis-ease" too close to home to acknowledge? Did they drape it in whispers of denial, head shaking, and puzzled frowns?

Did some relegate Virginia's pain to a lack of faith? Did they gossip or pray about her "condition"? Did she seem somehow spiritually off-limits for these extended periods? Or did the mothers of the children next door and down the street silently support her, dropping by at the back door with a homemade pie, a handful of peonies in June, daisies in July? Many of them had large families and heavy burdens, too. It was a time for stalwart women, but did anyone secretly wish they could hide away for a time like Virginia?

Expectations must have run high for this daughter of the founding pastor of their church who played the organ there on Sundays. Did the congregation allow for her human frailty? Of her six siblings, five went into the ministry or taught in church schools. What hidden pressures taunted this woman? Who played the church organ when she could not, or did the services continue without music? Did the longing for melody still rise in Virginia's soul, sequestered in her darkened bedroom?

Times have changed, and supportive systems exist for those seasons when our minds and bodies can take no more. I am my sister's keeper. We are our sisters' keepers. We hear Virginia's unspoken loss, and we sense her anguish. We know her as we know ourselves on our stooped-shoulder days, those afternoons when we dwell on unfulfilled longings. We acknowledge the same energy drain, times when we wonder how we've come to this moment and what we ought to do, times when our gifts taunt instead of fulfill.

Virginia's story cries out to us from the long ago, as does her daughter's. But one generation later, Grace had learned to recognize and verbalize her needs—she realized that her word for the moment was *help*, and summoned the courage to say it. That she managed a teensy bit of self-care out there on that primitive homestead, and that she smiles today, bespeaks courage and progress.

She survived, and now her face shines like a quiet candle in a gentle breeze. Happy to learn from her, I'm so very grateful for her unaffected wisdom, so glad for our connection. All around us are older women with experiences that might just supply the antidote we crave, and many of them would like nothing better than to share their stories.

Births

Lately, my thinking returns like a compass needle to the idea of our gifts. The parable of the talents brought up the subject in our Lectio Divina group the other day. What disturbs the reader is not that the man who buried his talent produced less than the others, but that he produced nothing at all.

Many of my writing students possess tremendous talent, but those with a natural ability often don't recognize it until they fulfill their first assignments. Why do human beings not recognize the gifts they possess? If we are to put our talents to use, why don't we automatically know what we have so we can be as productive as possible?

Why do so many of us spend so much time in the seeking process, slogging along, wondering what we have to offer? The desire to contribute can stymie as we blunder our way, unsure of our purpose. Doesn't this method waste our energies and our short time on earth?

This morning, I called a friend who's a bit overwhelmed with life right now. For several months, we've e-mailed about a joint writing project. In our conversation, she described the launching of our endeavor as a "birthing." My sentiments exactly—this urge to give birth to ideas festering in our minds resembles a delivery.

This morning, two days after Thanksgiving, cold windy snow arrived, an unwelcome intruder to arthritis sufferers, a happy friend to children at play. Such weather was made for boiling down a turkey carcass, stirring bones as they simmer in broth with a bit of added vinegar. In that bubbling state, vital nutrients transmute from bone to broth. The same type of process occurs with ideas in our minds.

Birthing will be my word today, as I reduce a turkey carcass to broth. I inhale the steam, pick the bones clean, and feel rejuvenated. Why not invite Grace over for tea? Who knows what insight she will offer?

Someone meeting this woman for the first time would greet a plain, rural, straightforward nonagenarian, yet having her as my guest motivates me to use cloth napkins and light three candles in the middle of the oak dining room table. The dining room table? Yes, at long last we have finished the floor, our table centered and ready for use. That's reason enough to celebrate.

Today, Grace bubbles over with her second child's birth story. She and Allan decided they would utilize the Osage Hospital this time. She laughs and exclaims, "Having a baby there in those days was like giving birth right out in the street."

With our heads full of the privacy and sanitation surrounding modern birthing, we enter her 1950 experience. Their firstborn, a son, was born across the border in Minnesota, since their farm lay near a town where Grace's sister worked as a nurse in the hospital. But Osage was a little closer, so they determined to head in that direction for the second baby.

The hospital, a big old white house on a residential street just a couple of blocks southwest of the county courthouse, served the townspeople and surrounding rural communities. The maternity ward, situated upstairs, consisted of several bedrooms with two beds each, and one bathroom that doubled as the delivery room. When a woman went into labor, the rest of the expectant or new mothers had no recourse but to wait outside until they heard a newborn cry.

Downstairs, nurses tended people with various diseases, and doctors performed necessary surgeries. The mother-to-be had to pass through this floor en route to the second floor delivery room. The whole scenario seems not quite possible—heavy with child, Grace climbed the stairs through who knows what contagion to this completely public room.

Giving birth in her lonely farmhouse doesn't seem like such a bad option. During her stay, four other women awaited their babies, and since Grace was overdue, the doctor attempted to induce labor.

During visiting hours, her roommate's husband occupied a chair when Grace's water broke. Modest and not one to create a stir, she waited in the soaked bed, hoping he would leave. When he lingered, she managed to pull herself up and into the dark closet, taking a clean gown and pads with her. Fumbling in the dark, she changed both and left the room in search of the doctor and nurse.

A woman whose husband carried her up the stairs after she fainted during labor pains occupied the bath-delivery room. As Grace arrived on the third floor, the doctor and nurse covered the woman's nose and mouth with a cloth containing ether from the ether can.

The same procedure awaited Grace—contractions had to be stopped, they believed, since someone else already laid claim to the birthing bed. The other woman had to wait until the delivery room opened up, and not until her baby had arrived could Grace deliver.

The actual delivery seems like an aside. On top of everything, women normally stayed in this hospital for six to nine days to recover.

"Many doctors had just come back from the War," Grace explains when I shudder at the use of ether and the encouragement to bottle-feed rather than nurse infants. "It was still better than having the baby at home because at least the doctor was there."

I wonder. At any rate, the second offspring survived. Now Grace and Allan had a boy and a girl.

One more baby, unplanned, would enter their family, an exuberant surprise when Grace turned forty-two. Realizing the undeniable symptoms of pregnancy and, as always, seeing the positive side, she mentioned her condition to Allan one day.

"It's all in your head, woman," the grizzled farmer pronounced, now fifty years old. When Grace began to show, he remarked that he would be seventy when this baby turned twenty.

Indeed, he would be dying of cancer on this son's twentieth birthday. But the little one proved a mighty gift, full of delights for the whole family to enjoy. Taking him to school on the first day of kindergarten, this older mom stood out as more of a grandmother figure among the mothers in the elementary schoolyard. I'm betting she spared them some parental sorrows because of the leadership, positive outlook, and kindness she still exhibits today.

My mother may have looked the same on her youngest's first day of kindergarten when I was twenty-three. Of course, Grace's birthing tale makes me think of Mom this afternoon and wonder if she endured such a crazy hospital scenario.

Hearing about Mom's deliveries would have been fun, but she disclosed few details. The subject of childbirth, probably because of its connection to sex, always remained off-limits. She volunteered only one statement during one of my pregnancies when I asked about her deliveries.

"Mine were short and didn't really hurt that much."

Not everything can be compared, but enough similarities in age and situation exist between Grace and Mom that some sort of comfort weaves into my heart as I get to know Grace and hear her stories. Reading *Life on the Farm with Allan* and entering into Virginia's saga a generation earlier, ear bound to the Metropolitan Opera on Saturday afternoons, I think of Mom, too, doing the best she could.

No music lessons graced her childhood. She'd never learned to read music, but she loved it. Taking me to town every week on Saturday afternoons for a piano lesson took courage when money was scarce. Maybe even my beginner's playing helped to fill her artistic bent, like Virginia's operas.

Often Mom would yell a request into the piano room as I pounded away. I wonder what thoughts and feelings she entertained during our annual recitals. I'd like to think she experienced satisfaction and hope. Did she escape during those two recital hours each spring in the Congregational church? One spring, she sang in an Easter Cantata, which required driving through winter snows on icy roads to practice one night a week. For years after that, she would hum some of those songs.

For her, reading the Sunday paper may have paralleled

Virginia's opera times. The weekly state newspaper arrived early in the morning, delivered to our farmyard by a man from town. With a big Sunday dinner to prepare, kids to dress for Sunday school, and—when she wasn't pregnant or caring for a little one—herself to get ready for church, afternoon was her time to read the paper.

She read it as if there were no tomorrow. We would stand a foot from her as she pored over the pages, demanding attention by repeating, "Mom!" until she finally responded. Sometimes we had to say the word four times before she'd look up through glazed eyes.

"What do you *want*?" When we were older, we laughed at this, especially when she ignored us completely.

Now I realize, meager as this small contact with the outside world seems, the Sunday paper fed her hunger for words, for learning, for something more. Women commonly lost themselves in home and family during those years, but at least Mom took one weekly time for herself.

In this place, this time, these three women come together to meet my need. As I seek to develop and use my gifts, they surround me with the tangible sense that I'll be all right, that guilt will loosen its grip on my soul. One day I will see the cup half full in my relationship with Mom.

The fears and dreams of the four of us intertwine through the generations in a sense of purpose. These women stand with me in this unique house, in this unique season of life.

Our housing search in this town was disappointing. I had in mind a big square home with a front porch and an open staircase, and wouldn't have minded if God threw in a fireplace and a hot tub. But no such houses bore For Sale signs. In fact, this one sat empty for five years, still not officially for sale when we started looking. Through word-of-mouth, we learned that the owner might consider selling.

My idealized notions didn't include such hard work to make a place livable. I saw us moving right in and arranging our furniture on lovely hardwood floors. But God had another plan. Well into our renovation, several houses appeared on the market that fit my original prayer, and I didn't handle it so well.

"Why couldn't that house have been for sale when we came here to look?" Groan.

But now some time has passed, and one consistent message filters into my reluctant ears and heart. No other house in town has this one's history. No other house could have led me into such a relationship with Grace. And to my knowledge, no other house has such an accessible, three-generation story. And story is, in the final analysis, the best gift.

Perhaps I wouldn't have been unable to take it all in at an earlier time. Perhaps the juxtaposition of former inhabitants with who I am and who I want to be wraps the gift I've longed to open. It took some time, but my fidgety heart has now mellowed enough to receive.

The Long-range View

Allan died at seventy from the toll of heavy smoking, and Grace now lives a few blocks from her birthplace, in a spacious, well-kept home with a wonderful pillared front porch. She spends her time out there in summer, and I ride my bike over to chat with her. Since her eyesight has failed, friends drive her to church and other activities.

Her children and grandchildren call and visit, and several young women in the community frequent her house for her indefatigable cheerleading. Her friend Marcia was right—her life is beautiful. When Grace answers my questions about the old days, vivid stories well up. On every visit, some fresh perspective on a significant aspect of life accompanies her words, and she always seems surprised when I thank her for what she has taught me.

The latest incident she shared occurred in 1952, a summer that held such promise. Her petunias bloomed early, the garden grew like a rainforest, and she and Allan maintained high hopes for a glorious harvest. Then a devastating hailstorm hit.

Ascending from the basement, where she and their three children weathered the "gray whirling fury," she joined Allan at the window. In this fourth year of farming, they put intense energy into preparing and planting the fields and garden.

Grace clutched her sweater. Out in the yard, her strawberry bed swam in ice and water. Ice lay in drifts, the corn crop beaten into sodden stumps. The oats, prematurely threshed by the storm, lay in the fields, useless.

The little family huddled together, dismayed. But the next morning at Sunday services their pastor offered a prayer for the hail victims.

"Somehow we didn't feel quite so smitten and alone. In the

next weeks, the insurance adjusters made a generous settlement on the corn crop. We had no insurance on the beans and oats, but a friend offered us bedding straw for the cattle."

Fifty-four years later, this survivor still models positive thinking. The storms she weathered remind me to be tenacious and thankful in a culture that exalts perfection. Technological advances have changed our perceptions and expectations so that contentment seems inappropriate unless things go exactly as planned or predicted.

But imperfection reigns. We do our best, yet situations don't always work out. Sometimes relationships crumble, portfolios fail, projects languish, our dreams lie dormant, and our prayers fail to blossom into reality. Even so, a thankful attitude can still be the warm lining in our coats.

"Out in the corn fields imperceptibly, day by day, a little miracle took place as summer wore on. Tattered leaves lifted, stalks started growing, ears pushed out and we knew there would be a little crop after all. It wasn't the thick sturdy growth of other years, but no corn ever looked better. Petunias sent out new shoots and became a mass of blooms. Ours was a beautiful world once more.

"Along with this I noticed that Allan, tense and tired before the hail, became once more the easy-going man I married. With enough cash from the insurance to tide us over, and part of a crop to look forward to, he was able to relax. Somehow, come drought, come storm, I couldn't worry about our crops any more. We would do our part, and God always does His part."

"The luxury is simply being alive," a soldier during World War II wrote from Germany's Hurtgen Forest after a vicious battle with no clear winner and incalculable human loss. Simply being alive qualified as luxury. My goal is to see life from such a vantage point, and Grace's example cheers me on.

Broth and Wholeness

"Ninth grade girls come in all shapes and sizes. Some like a featherbed, full of fluff, others like a stick, and some full-figured. I didn't like teaching home economics to this age group," Grace spouts. "They could jam up those old pedal sewing machines faster than a person could fix them."

Grace's patience far exceeds mine, but hearing her describe working with adolescent girls as a struggle redoubles my conviction that certain professions require a call to martyrdom. After student teaching in a junior high school, I felt certain that instructing at that age level demands a distinct vocation.

At home after her marriage, her teaching days over, Grace used her sewing skills to patch overalls, using the 4-H patch which other women in the area thought too newfangled. The newfangled aspect involved using a sewing machine rather than one's hands to push a needle through thick denim.

When expecting her third child, she couldn't safely complete the up-and-down foot action necessary to pedal the treadle machine, so the overalls suffered during this time, but otherwise, the 4-H patch served Grace's family well. She cut a hole into each worn knee, slit all four corners so that a piece of fabric from the leg of another overall could be slipped into the hole, then stitched a careful, straight line around the edge.

Stacks of painstaking, monotonous work, but in contrast to spending hours with a needle and thimble stitching the lines by hand, it must have seemed like a breeze (as Grace would say).

A breeze. Let this remarkable woman's viewpoint osmosis into me.

She accepted her duties, and they contributed to the sense of purpose women felt about their work. She woke with prescribed jobs, and went to sleep with a sense of satisfaction.

Today, many women find such satisfaction in careers outside the home. Then, with time at a premium, they feel driven to accomplish everyday chores. But when the children lead their own adult lives, an underlying assurance of purpose can dissipate. More than one empty nester has experienced this.

What is our purpose? Grace knew hers: chief supporter of her husband, nurturer of her children, the adhesive holding their home together. Her patches protected their knees with pride, and her prayers protected their spirits. Her devotion to her family and her diligence shone out from the lonely countryside all the way to Marcia's home a day's travel away.

Soul Sustenance

"He restores my soul." The Twenty-third Psalm, so familiar but relegated to grief in our culture, deserves more attention. We need its balm not only when someone has died, but during the pangs of everyday life. Of all the active verbs in this Psalm's outline of God's care for us, the word *restores* takes precedence for me today as we restore this old house.

Never one to buy a can of factory-produced broth, I gladly spend intermittent portions of an entire winter day nursing a bunch of chicken bones into hearty liquid, the medicinal faculties of which have been lauded for generations, and more recently cited in scientific research.

Neither Mom nor Grandma taught me this. Maybe they both had far too much to do. During my first job after college, a co-worker's wife explained her habit of simmering a chicken on the back burner the whole day.

Often, a cooked chicken provides far too much broth for present needs, so I freeze containers for future bouts with colds or sore throats. Weak with fever some later day, I'll be able to thaw this miracle soup base and imbibe healing properties from a steaming cup.

With seven children born in this house, Virginia must certainly have relied on chicken broth during cold and flu seasons. Once, the front door bore a quarantine sign because one of the children contracted scarlet fever. Grace describes the situation with a hearty chuckle. The proximity of the elementary school playground probably contributed to the quarantine sign, although this household was one of many sporting such a public warning.

Accepting the sign posted on the front door, Virginia went in search of her sick child, Ben, a lively seven-year-old. Eventually she discovered him not in the house, but down the street playing on a coaster wagon with some neighbor children. She grew so weary of children being sick, she put one of the younger boys in bed with the others so he could become infected, thereby accelerating the process.

Grace giggles. He was the only sibling who never did contract scarlet fever.

A few weeks ago our adult son called to say he was coming down with a sinus infection. "I'd make you some chicken broth if I were there," I responded.

"I'm doing that as we speak, Mom." I must have done something right.

In other kinds of pain, restoration also follows nurturing. Loss and transition require thoughtful care. The turn-around comes in voicing our pain, and then our wounded hearts, in time, can heal. We all remember feeling as though we will never smile or laugh again.

Silently, slowly, the warmth of friendship, the work of remembering, the appropriation of resources and acceptance of ourselves as fallible, frail beings bring comfort and restoration. The broth of spiritual and emotional healing takes time to work. Like restoring an old house, renewing our inner strength requires commitment, yet we do not work alone.

"He restores my soul." Especially during deeply disturbing family troubles, hope treads with a small step. Gradually, we gain strength enough to stand without succumbing to guilt's relentless ravages or to denial's deterrents. Imbued with power to breathe again, straighten our shoulders and carry on, we waste no more of life in dead-ended journeys into closed-door places.

We stop trying to fix the unfixable. We ruminate on God's restorative powers rather than our learned coping mechanisms. We unlearn some tactics, and rest in our Creator's abilities rather than relying on our perceived ones.

We claim our gifts anew, and little by little, put aside our bent toward second-guessing. Each day promises productivity and regeneration. How good it seems, once again, to step into the sunshine, claim our place, and live our lives. We start out all over again.

Trying

"You need to stop trying. Try is your middle name." The counselor could see the woman was a controller, and things were getting out of control.

"Instead of figuring this out in your mind and attempting to persuade people to conform to your plan, simply state how you feel."

"How I feel?" But her upbringing forbade that kind of honesty. If she felt lonely, neglected by the spouse who vowed to love her, surely she couldn't come right out and say so.

"If you feel lonely, tell him. Then, don't try to fix the situation. Take a walk. Let him sit with his discomfort. Let him own it. He's an adult. He can change, but only if he knows what's wrong and is allowed to deal with it without your intervention."

Major food for thought. When I first heard this story, I had no idea how much trying stood in the way of emotional and spiritual health.

"Come unto Me, and I will give you..." Something to fix? Not.

But the other word, the one Jesus used—rest—escaped me. I had trouble sleeping, as well as trouble letting go of things. Trained to try at all costs, I badgered my way ahead, confident that with enough effort, something good would result. It was unnatural to believe "all would be well."

A friend of mine puts it so well: "I traded a work and performance-centered childhood and youth for a work and performance-centered Christian experience. Then (duh), I did the same thing in marriage and parenting. Hello? Earth to Ellie?"

No, it's actually heaven to Ellie. The idea of rest smells of heaven. Did I think I brought hope to my Creator's heart by managing life instead of living it? Did this method bring joy to me? Hardly. It kept me so busy managing things—and emotions—that I couldn't simply live. And neither could my husband or children.

Little by little, rest becomes more than an idea. As I rest in the word for this day, my galloping mind comes a bit more under control. If I can sustain this practice, who knows? I might make it through twenty-four hours someday without taking things into my hands that belong in someone else's.

Recently, I met a woman whose trials astound me. Her husband, diagnosed with Asperger's syndrome, wants nothing to do with a shared life. He stares at a spot on the table when they eat, never inquires about any part of her life, drops all family responsibilities on her shoulders, and rejects any form of intimacy. But this woman's mother and in-laws blame her for his behavior. Does that sound familiar?

She sent me a poem by an anonymous author that describes her marriage. Each line details unfulfilled hopes and dreams, loneliness, isolation, rejection, disillusionment, grief, and a sense nothing will ever change. She wonders if prolonging such pain is "God's will" and brings joy to Him.

When we consider Allan's attitudes toward Grace's desperate need and her pleas for running water, some resemblances surface. Of course, we don't know the details of their daily lives, and they lived in a time when a man could exhibit sheer self-centered ego without any recourse. The wife simply zipped her lips and trudged on. Try, try, try.

So I ponder: though seeing the cup half full is a positive trait, does unceasing effort to meet a husband's needs and hold a family together even if your own needs go unmet please our Heavenly Father? Does Grace's "Allan was so overworked, it's understandable that he couldn't find time to pipe water to the house," exemplify a joyous Christian woman's testimony of perseverance and love, or of trying to the death under unfair circumstances that shout selfishness?

Sixty years after her specific trials, possibly it's easier for her to see the positives. Marriage gave her children and grandchildren, and with them, purpose. But how long should a modern woman with a tragic, draining relationship, and with alternatives unavailable in Grace's time, keep on trying? Perhaps she has taken as her word, "Come to Me."

And she *does* come to Jesus—over and over and over. She has for years. Decades. But nothing has changed. She meant her vows when she said them, and does not take commitment lightly. After all, *in sickness and in health, till death us do part.*

No, we are not to copy the patterns of our culture, where faithfulness has taken a back seat to personal fulfillment at any cost. But could this wife's Creator intend her marriage vow to result in severe depression, her children's long-term dis-ease, or even in her own untimely death? Does the Christian concept of marital faithfulness require losing the life she was created to live?

Oppression

A few years ago, I wrote the benediction that begins this section at a churchwomen's conference where I facilitated a grief and loss workshop. This particular denomination provided a lovely women's retreat atmosphere, and I was excited to be a part of the gathering. But as I read the benediction to close the retreat, the last line caught in my throat. "May the God of YOU empower you."

What I'd witnessed during the weekend showed me gigantic obstacles to that happening for this group of beautiful women. To experience God's empowerment, they would have to take a gigantic leap of faith at great risk.

My attention monitor moved from interested to incredulous as the retreat proceeded. I had no idea these Christian women quavered under such legalism. When people have a chance to express long-held grief, emotions release in great lumps, like swallowed stones. Sometimes an actual choking sensation accompanies the outpouring.

In a gorgeous setting surrounded by millions of perfect photo-op scenes, heavy groves of tall pin oaks and soft maples shimmering in the sunlight, God's women sat in my grief and loss workshop. I thought few would come, but many did. Some were unable to verbalize their oppression, but for others, the time was right and the place seemed safe.

When terrible loss comes in the shadow of religiosity, complications increase. Held down by injunctions from both the church and their "Christian" husbands, participants' grim tales gripped everyone in the room.

My heart sickened at their outpourings. How could outwardly righteous men who say they believe in the God of the Bible so rigorously control their wives and children? Sheathed with misinterpreted Bible passages, they stab the life out of their loved ones, people given them by God to protect and love. Theirs is a severe faith, devoid of mercy. I left the retreat stunned and heavy in spirit.

Sometimes, stricken with the selfishness and stupidity of human beings, we can only shake our heads and hold people before God for intervention. These fragile daughters of the Heavenly Father, trapped in what passes for truth, cannot be freed by the likes of me, although I wanted to run into the beautiful retreat center and scream, "They have a right to be on earth, as much as any of their oppressive husbands!" Of course, that would have accomplished nothing but an earlier trip to the airport.

And so, the last line of my benediction, a prayer that God would empower these women, choked me up. Empowerment involves many steps. First, we must acknowledge our soul hunger, and then desire to respond regardless of the consequences. This entails traveling deep enough into God's unconditional love to believe that He placed the desire for wholeness and liberty within us.

In the process, we can become beneficent to ourselves. It's a long road from harsh self-judgment to merciful kindness. Many of us consistently show kindness to others and refrain from judging, but when it comes to our own attitudes and actions, rude condemnation reigns. Cutting ourselves some slack takes time and practice. Unfortunately, each encounter with a controller reinforces the tendency to discount and dishonor our own autonomy.

Manipulation and abuse have a cumulative effect. Controllers know how to angle us off-center a bit more with each confrontation. With enough time, we feel helpless and can't even put into words why we feel confused or upset. Of course, this looks like evidence that the controller is right about us, but we can learn to recognize that off-kilter sensation as a warning sign, our body telling us that something is wrong.

Defining others invalidates them. We know what we saw, said, or felt. When someone else contradicts our perception and knowledge, this amounts to a loss of love. They reject the real person we are, and of course, leave no room for growth into who God desires us to become. If we allow another to continue to define us, we also lose our self.

"You always..." When someone begins a statement with *You*, they attempt to define. But God gives us each of us the task of defining ourselves, not others.

The trouble is, many women grow up deferring to someone else's opinion, and if they marry, they trust their spouse, never thinking the partner may have an agenda that does not include the "real them." Trivializing feelings and opinions amounts to an attack on a person created in God's image, someone God highly values. How can a woman maintain her integrity as an autonomous human being with a constant onslaught declaring her thinking and emotions flawed?

We have learned to doubt ourselves, so moving back toward the integrity of our personhood happens slowly and only with great resolve. If a woman is married to a church leader or pillar of the community, the confusion and humiliation can be insurmountable without professional help.

Standing up for oneself results from knowing that our emotions and conclusions make sense. This is the dignity of personhood. Story after story comes out of Al-Anon and other such organizations as individuals realize that other people share similar experiences. They are not crazy. They can trust their own intuition that something is amiss in a relationship, no matter what the other party asserts. Our intuition is God's unique gift to each human being.

The day a woman takes up her own cause is a red-letter day! No longer will she abandon her own spirit. No longer will the Old Testament admonition "Walk humbly with your God" mean she must put aside her talents, skills, and dreams. True humility—descending from the pedestal of judging herself and others—will now soften her harshness. No longer will anyone shortchange her by saying she "doesn't understand; always complains; can't take a joke; jumps to conclusions; or blows things out of proportion." She can define herself, thank you very much.

No longer will this woman equate humility with ignoring her own needs while attending to others'. She will measure humility by her willingness to build her relationship with God, not by how much she does for the people around her. Walking humbly, she will place all her loved ones' needs in God's hands instead of trying to fix things. She will abdicate the throne of being responsible for everything and everyone. This woman will seek to learn what "letting go" means as she lives in the knowledge that her truth matters and deserves as much attention as anyone else's.

All of this and more I would have liked to breathe into the participants at that retreat. I would have liked to say, "You are worthy. God intends a future of freedom and joy for you, and you can come out of this. Your feelings, neither good nor bad, are worth consideration. You can come to honor yourself as your Creator does, and as you do, you can learn to stand up for yourself."

But such pronouncements cannot transform lifetime patterns. Prayer can, though, along with the Holy Spirit's painstaking work of waking us from sleep, nudging us from apathy, and empowering us from within.

Avon Calling

A friend's mother took him to see her gravestone in a small town cemetery. Her engraving ranks right up there for creativity.

Avon Calling, the inscription reads. In her eighties, this woman still sold Avon products.

"I was going to have them write 'Ding, Dong. Avon Calling,' but everyone around here already thinks I'm a ding dong, so I just did the last two words."

Quel panache!

How do some people survive life's ups and downs to remain so vibrant? Some of us wonder how we'll find the strength for another decade, while certain others seem to thrive, their capacity for engaging the present moment adding years to their lives.

Recently a woman of ninety-one described her neighbor's response to a minor crisis in their small apartment complex. The two of them were checking out a rosebush still wrapped for protection from the harsh winter when they spied a nest of newborn wild bunnies inside the enclosure.

Her neighbor gave her a look. "Go in and get some water, Helen." Helen obeyed, knowing the tiny creatures would meet a quick and simple death.

"We really had no choice," she explained as I gulped down shock and disbelief. "Rosie and I couldn't just let those bunnies take over our yard and eat our bushes!"

These women have survived tough times, and probably never heard of PETA. As children of the Great Depression, during their years of childrearing, they did what they had to do. Problems couldn't wait. They kept a gun handy for emergencies and allotted no time for philosophical contemplation. And now, in their own little yard, the two of them protected their rosebushes.

Many widows live alone in our town and manage well. After church today, another stalwart soul, ninety-two, told me she enjoyed reading my newspaper articles.

"I did have to look up a couple of words in the dictionary, though."

"Oh, really? Which ones?" I asked her. She remembered the exact context.

Maybe this community has more than the national average of totally "together" elderly women. They provide quite a role model. How can I complain about my everyday challenges with them around, taking care of business?

Purpose

This morning I had tea with a woman whose daughter is a cheerleading coach in a large midwestern city. This would-be cheerleader always came just below the last person chosen for the high school squad.

In college, she decided she had nothing to lose, so she tried out. In a delightful twist, her name appeared on the list, so she cheered all through her college career. Now, she teaches others how. When I asked what kinds of teams her daughter's groups support, the woman said, "None."

That's right, these cheerers don't support teams. They cheer for the sake of cheering. I'd never thought of cheerleading as an end, but these teams compete in a national championship. The purpose lies in the cheering, not in a team's success. Why not?

A few years ago on a flight from Wichita to Minneapolis, I had the express joy of sitting next to a Canadian Egyptian Orthodox Christian. Somehow we got on the subject of praying to the saints. I still think often of his reply to my clearly Protestant question, "Do you pray to the saints?"

"Of course!" he replied. When asked to explain this practice, he launched into the topic with exuberance.

"Do you ever ask your friends to pray for you?"

I nodded.

"Well, believers who've gone before us want us to do well. They're our friends, cheering us on." He alluded to the eleventh chapter of Hebrews, and his practical application made sense. Sometimes people in what we label "ritualistic churches" take Scripture as literally as fundamentalists.

"Calling a friend who lives nearby or across the country to pray for us during a particularly trying time or asking one of our friends already in Heaven to pray is all the same." He smiled at me as if sharing a valuable family secret.

"Now do you understand?"

Yes, I did. And it seems to me that, although my strict Protestant ancestors would squawk, there might be some spiritual power here that we miss out on. What could be so wrong with having extra prayers? What kinds of comfort and joy might we lack by not accessing the concern of saints on the other side?

My picture of heaven has always focused on constant worship and praise of our Creator and Savior. But what if the "communion of saints" is more literal, with those already in heaven desiring to be involved with Christians on earth? If, as my seatmate assured me, this viewpoint stems back to the ancient Church, then vast segments of Christians suffer loss.

But some lines of theological thought label as sin any connection with the saints. I've heard the name-calling from several quarters.

My seatmate adamantly refuted the objection that asking for help from anyone but Christ amounts to idol worship. His unequivocal, "Jesus is the sole advocate for us with the Father," sprang from sincere faith in our preeminent Savior.

This Coptic Christian referred not to salvation, but to our daily spiritual walk. He spoke of God's provision in light of our intrinsic need for support. How would adherence to his belief affect our sense of purpose? Knowing that moment by moment, unseen heavenly cheerleaders observe the victories and defeats of our earthly passage, how might our worldview change?

Does life get any more purposeful than being a part of God's eternal family, bound together by the Spirit, whether in heaven or on earth? Depression and discouragement run rampant among modern believers—surely any increase in our sense of purpose would be worth a little theological adjustment. How long has it been since we meditated on the word *cheer*?

I have a friend who invokes the saints, whom she describes as her friends. Saint Christopher for travel, Saint Luke for physicians, Saint Anthony for the poor and those who search for lost things. She grins as she mentions Saint Anthony's name.

"Depending on the need, that's who I ask for help. I invoke Saint Anthony when searching for lost things and when I'm lost, like 'Okay Tony, I don't know where I am. Even my GPS is puzzled. Help me find the correct street.'"

For her, sharing requests with the saints is no different from asking you to pray for me. It isn't praying to God directly, but when I ask you to pray for me, I don't ask you to be my Savior, only to intercede on my behalf.

My friend says, "That's what the saints do. I ask them to please talk to God since I know they care about my needs and are near to /him."

Inevitable Protestant protests emerge: "Christ loved us enough to die for us. Why do we need someone else to intercede for us? Jesus, the one mediator between God and man, invites us to bring our requests straight into God's presence. Why mess around with a saint?"

My Egyptian seatmate calmly considered all these questions with grace. With Christ unquestionably his Savior and Lord, the saints' prayers on his behalf still comfort him in his earthly struggles.

What if God means the comfort found in a relationship with the saints for all of His children, Protestants included? What is "the communion of the saints," if not this?

Did Virginia and Grace miss out on some valuable communion during their trials due to their Protestantism? Grace fought with depression as she carried heavy water pails from the pump house to the barn. Wouldn't her heart have lightened to know the saints cheered her on?

Mom comes to mind as well. What if she stands along the path of the race I run? What if she roots for me instead of concurring with that inner condemning voice that tells me I failed her? What if Grandma, too, watches, saying, "Don't be so hard on yourself. You've got a lot of living yet to do, and your gifts will come to fruition. Don't give up!"

This line of thought brings me back to "For All The Saints." Why didn't I see it before? "...yet all are one, within Thy grand design. Allelujah, Allelujah."

My Egyptian Christian friend's face beamed as he spoke of his own personal "communion with the saints." What right do I have to condemn his faith as heretical? My insignificant ruminations will change no diehard Protestant's mind, but that's not my goal. I worry less and less about doctrinal correctness. Is that such a bad trend?

Part Four

One of the religion scholars came up. Hearing the lively exchanges of question and answer and seeing how sharp Jesus was in his answers, he put in his question: “Which is most important of all the commandments?”

Jesus said, “The first in importance is, ‘Listen Israel: The Lord your God is one; so love the Lord God with all your passion and prayer and intelligence and energy.’ And here is the second: ‘Love others as well as you love yourself.’ There is no other commandment that ranks with these.”

The religion scholar said, “A wonderful answer, Teacher! So lucid and accurate – that God is one and there is no other. And loving him with all passion and intelligence and energy, and loving others as well as you love yourself. Why, that’s better than all offerings and sacrifices put together!”

When Jesus realized how insightful he was, he said, “You’re almost there, right on the border of God’s kingdom.”

After that, no one else dared ask a question.

~ Mark 12, MSG

It Is

It is the Lord. "It is the Lord who has made us, and not we ourselves," proclaims Psalm 100. "Your old way of life was nailed to the cross," adds Romans, chapter six. The ancient Psalms meet the Cross... it's all about the Lord. It *is* the Lord.

That means it's not anyone else, or in Jesus's words, "there is no other." We struggle with turning over command of our destinies to God, our Higher Power. We've administrated our lives for years, with varying degrees of success. But due to crises beyond our control, the concept of submission now looms like a storm cloud.

For some, the battle lies in forsaking the outdated unconscious coping mechanisms—denial, control, shame, enabling, fear, blame—which kept us alive in our youth. These methods once ensured our safety, and in adulthood, still masquerade as helpers. They so infiltrate our being that we need help to recognize them.

Crises force us to ask the truly difficult questions. Who am I, really, apart from my coping strategies? When it all comes down, do I rest in the Jesus I proclaim to worship?

We must acknowledge the hard truths and win deliverance from false powers before wholeness can come. In spite of determined attempts to leave these impostors at the Cross, we discover them resurrected, vying for their old role of directing our lives.

For example, if fear has reigned for decades, stepping out with faith in God's ability to transform can be difficult. As children, we learned to distrust, since our very survival depended on caution. As adults, we move into uncharted territory with great hesitation, accompanied by intense striving to "help" God reorder our lives. Our supposed "aid" only complicates the process, but we blunder on.

Accepting that we have anything worthwhile to offer is tough when repeated negative messages rained down upon us during childhood and adolescence. Perhaps God might take us in, but use us? Impossible! How dare we think that we could ____? Fill in the blank with anything worthwhile: write a book, sing a song, seek a new career, parent with hope, pursue a long-held dream. Yet our Father urges us forward into wholeness disguised as risk.

Our childhood safety depended on carefulness. How, then, can we depend on One so totally unknown? We've always felt responsible for everything and everyone...what does giving ourselves into the care and protection of another entail? Our heads pop up out of our holes like prairie dogs in this new land of opportunity, constantly alert for danger.

Our teacher has inconceivable patience. We know our giftedness comes from Him, but we find myriad excuses to stay in the shadows, since moving into the light means attracting attention and the horrible possibility of pride. We have enough sins to deal with already. Why risk pride?

Then, somewhere along the way, we discover that pride camouflages itself as mock humility. The whole world still revolves around me if I'm calling the shots, attempting to appear small and "nice." What if my Creator *wants* me in a certain amount of limelight?

"It is the Lord who has made us" brings hope. After a lifetime of believing we could change others' attitudes or actions, at the same time we gave away our personal power. "It is the Lord" fills us with relief. Creating, living, forgiving, healing, changing, growing...all of these originate outside us.

Someone ever-present, ever-loving, all-knowing, and gently powerful is untouched by any variety of human coping mechanism we can concoct. Thank God, it is not us. It is the Lord.

My three-year-old grandson watched as I mourned the

loss of my daffodils, set to burst into glorious color. Last night, temperatures dropped into the teens. Proud stalks crusted with cold, snapped in my fingers. Burgeoning yellow potential hung limp on fragile stems. I took some of them inside, in the slim hope that water would revive them. Nope. Green mush filled the vase.

Tender-eyed, my grandson listened as I explained. This sensitive little guy had waited with me through the long winter for the flowers' regeneration.

"Grandma," he announced as he patted my arm. "I'll fix them for you. I'll go and get my dad's tools and make them better again."

Right. This strong-minded, sweet little fellow could as much "fix" my daffodils as we can make right our torn, stiffened lives. Oh, as humans we certainly try, until finally, breathless and exhausted with our efforts, we slip into this word: "It is the Lord."

Empowerment

Al-Anon principles rest on trusting in our Higher Power. Viewing ourselves as valuable is foundational to an autonomous life. Again today, I'm drawn to the phrase, *It is the Lord.*

Yesterday I contemplated the story of a man who acts as his own god. He wouldn't admit to this, but as he exerts control over his realm, which shrinks with age, he acts as creator and sustainer of his personal universe. His wife recently began to recognize his demeaning attitude.

His wishes have always taken precedence over hers. How did she fall into such a victim state that permits someone else to make her decisions, limit her friends, even tell her what clothes to purchase? If she lived under the reign of a tyrannical religion, it would be easier to understand, but hers is a Christian family in the "land of the free."

How do individuals who assume the role of God get that idea? Enablers look so innocent, but they help these god-figures function. They think their actions keep things from falling apart, when they actually prevent others from learning. In this way, they contribute to the "godhood" of the abuser. Watchful always, they make sure the family image remains unstained while the god-person continues to resist change.

Since none of us controls anything in this life, we marvel at the degree of delusion involved in assuming we serve as master of another human being. Memoir-writing classes produce all manner of stories, but one that recently captured my attention provides a vivid example of domination.

A mother from a bygone generation still perseveres from the grave. So controlling that she would not allow her children to choose their own careers, she single-handedly robbed the world. How could she do this, and how could her husband stand by and watch? Not even one of her three offspring dared refuse her will. I'm grateful not to have known her.

In another case, a gentle older man's mother prevented him from marrying, because no girl ever met her approval. The man took care of her until she died, then lived alone until his death, but he would have made a great dad and grandfather. What a tragic waste!

Yet no one controls us unless we allow it. What sort of character weakness motivates us to afford another human being such power? Galatians five speaks of self-control as a fruit of the Spirit. Some people must control their need to control. Others of us must learn to control our passiveness in order to bear our distinct kingdom fruit.

Have I strayed from ruminating about God being God? I don't think so. All of our jumbled relationships originate from the false premise that someone other than God is God. To acknowledge the Almighty, to allow Him supremacy in our lives, solves the majority of our problems.

"Let go and let God," the saying goes, but when we've limped along under a demagogue's regime, letting go isn't easy. And limped along is accurate. One day we wake up to realize the crippling effect of our false loyalty. The amazing discovery that God does exactly the opposite of what our former ruler did, letting us be the "me" we were meant to be, takes some adjustment.

God will have none of our feeble victim pose. In this kingdom, the ruler desires and knows what is best, yet refuses to demand involuntary compliance. When God reigns, love becomes the banner of the day. We begin to step into our places as His children. This signifies true empowerment: the source of all strength shares His very power with us.

God is God. What an infinite concept to embrace. God is God and, wonder of wonders, desires us to be ourselves. Sometimes we think we must become like the messengers God used in the Scriptures, like Elijah, Queen Esther, or the Apostle Paul.

It rarely occurs to us that God wants us to be the unique person He created. After all, isn't this what it means to be created in the Creator's image? I was a slow learner. How could God's plan mean I was meant to be myself?

Slowly, I began to understand. Since God, who created us after His own likeness, is completely satisfied in being Himself, it stands to reason that He would desire our autonomy. It's not selfish or proud or any of the sins our inner voices accuse of, to accept who we are and live our lives. It is the Lord, and by the merciful grace of God, it is me.

God Indeed

"The Lord your God is indeed God, in heaven above and on earth below."
~ Joshua 2:11 (NRSV)

God is God. Indeed. Of course, isn't this truth obvious? Not for people who have known human tyranny. When one person in a family system claims absolute authority, the other members, trained from birth to bow and submit, have no idea that God indeed is God.

Walking on tiptoe is a hard habit to break. Painful physical, emotional, and verbal punishment results in careful watchfulness, lest we rock the boat. Mistakes prove our "boss" is right: we are worthless, stupid, and hopelessly flawed.

Gut-level instincts are rejected unless they harmonize with the dictator's views, so we learn to distrust ourselves. Here's a simple example from my childhood. One day I stayed home from school with the flu. My head hurt, I felt nauseous, and my energy level plummeted.

My dad taunted me, "You're just faking. You're not really sick." Maybe I should add that in the fifties, farmers worked very hard from planting to harvest, but in the winter, spent more time in the house. In my experience, January and February bring angst to farm families.

Even though I loved school and would much rather have been there than at home, his words worked on my spirit. I started doubting what my body told me. Those doubts didn't stop when I left home. It's still difficult for me to listen to the physical signs that tell me to take a break.

Entering a kingdom of love takes time. Trust develops gradually and only with repeated practice. It's tough to trust a God you cannot see when your model for God teaches you by word and deed to distrust yourself.

This word *indeed* seems nonessential to the meaning of Joshua's sentence. Why not simply "the Lord your God is God"? Perhaps because the people needed "indeed," as we often need "really."

Really? We ask for clarification or assurance. Indeed? For sure. Absolutely. Definitely. Irrevocably. This one word, *indeed*, reveals the speaker's indelible intent. Do you get it, people? Indeed?

Love and authority mix easily in this kingdom, but not until we move beyond our frail understanding, encumbered and confused by our early teachings. How will we ever arrive at a safe emotional place where fear gives way to our God's exotic, perfect love, to a space where the God of both love and justice brings peace?

We arrive step by step as He carries us. Fragile lambs, wrapped in a protective, transforming cloak of grace eventually learn to walk on their own. Indeed does not imply instant. In the spiritual realm, rather, it implies surety.

Responsibility and Rest

One of the best calling card mottos I've read goes like this:

> Do not feel totally, personally, irrevocably responsible for everything. That's my job.
>
> Love,
>
> God

In the middle of a renovation, it's natural to feel personally responsible for everything. Today I turned on the Shop Vac only to have volumes of dust spray into the room. I was trying to do six things at once and neglected to change the filter. This is a great way to make more work for myself.

My feet and back ached when I grabbed the cleaner. I needed to take a break, but no, I had to "fix" one more mess in order to mark one more job off my list. In the process, I slowed down the desperately desired progress.

The words "Do not feel responsible for everything" instructs many an adult whose "inner child" still slaves to accomplish the impossible. "Do not" reminds us of many New Testament instructions: "Do not fear; do not be anxious; do not let your heart be troubled."

Most of the time, human nature rebels against imperatives. Many of Jesus's "do nots" command us not to forego something we enjoy, but something that drives us crazy. One would think we would want relief from feeling responsible for everything. Why wouldn't we jump at the promise of a lighter load?

The answer has to do with habit, with what roles we unknowingly accepted as children, and ultimately with change. To be human is to fear and resist change, even change for the better.

Big shifts must occur before we're able or willing to set aside our hard labor, calm ourselves, and enter into rest. One woman in her seventies admits to still enabling her fifty-something brother.

"I know it seems ridiculous." She shakes her head. "But he'll always be like a son to me, you know, and I can't let him continue to fail."

As we join her in the head shaking, we identify, for we know that moving past this type of rescuing happens only by the grace of God. We long for the tranquility of stepping beyond outdated family requirements that we care for everyone, even at the expense of our own health and well-being, yet resist taking the step.

When the original command came to us sugarcoated in religious talk, "God wants you to love your brother now, honey," emancipation means even more. The transition will be even more complicated.

How empowering to claim responsibility only for ourselves, to stand up to inner voices of self-proclaimed authorities over our spirits. How glorious to assume management of our own lives, and to claim ownership of our God-given choices.

Though this transformation means liberty for us, it may not be so wonderful for others used to dealing with "such a nice lady." They have no trouble showing us how much we've disappointed them. We've "rocked the boat." We've lifted the rug under which nasty secrets have lurked for lifetimes, disturbed the status quo, or even worse, "the peace."

Could our behavior possibly be God's will? Isn't everyone supposed to get along, regardless of personal cost? What about loving our neighbors "as ourselves"?

Tyrants still behave like tyrants, though they bear the family crest and pretend to come in the name of peace. How did our Lord respond to people bent on controlling everyone and everything? Our "meek and mild" Jesus became incensed. He disregarded attempts to keep Him in line, whether they originated with the Pharisees, His family, or even His followers.

It would behoove us to re-read the Good News. As much as

He loved mother and father, Luke 3 declares that Jesus, even as a youth, reminded them of His own call from God. He must "be about His Father's business."

He steadfastly went about that business in spite of the Pharisees' threats. The Gospels reveal His undeterred attention to kingdom work even when His family waited outside (Mark 3), and even when His own disciples disagreed about His methods. Imagine Peter recoiling at Jesus's rebuke in Matthew 16. "Peter, get out of my way. Satan, get lost. You have no idea how God works" (MSG).

As adult believers, our goal is to embrace how God works. Losing ourselves in others' schemes or the roles foisted upon us hinders us. Listening to old voices and obeying messages from which His Son died to free us brings our Creator no glory.

In learning to respond to God's voice, we might bear shaming from those who will do anything to retain our "niceness." So be it. Jesus knew scorn well. Why couldn't He be "normal" like the rest of His family? Why was His mission so completely outside the box? Why did He have to speak truth? Why couldn't He just be nice?

Moving beyond these inner and outer foes, we come into the freedom of our inheritance as children of God. In His presence, all other rulers, expelled with the force of His Word, slink off into oblivion. We may spend some time in regret for lost years, but not for long, because we grow accustomed to a new way of life.

We respond to our Lord's ability as He enables us. We are responsible not for everything, but for ourselves. His clear-cut command to "love others AS we love ourselves," becomes our banner. Like our Lord, we may suffer the ire of those who reject our new persona, but we learn to focus on the word God gives us, and we enjoy times of rest.

As I look back over my journey thus far, that's what I longed for during my college years. It's what I craved as a young wife and mother. It's what I would have exchanged everything I owned to have when my children entered adolescence. I called it by other names—peace and serenity—but simply put, it was rest. That inner sense that no matter what, all was well.

Hmm...once I get the extra dust cleaned up in here, I may brew a cup of tea and sit outside for a while. Ravishing autumn colors beckon me.

Somebody

In Romans 9, Paul describes God's redemptive work as making somebodies out of nobodies. My word for today hopped right off the page. *Nobody*. Not anyone. Ruminating sometimes leads us to antonyms.

How can a nonentity become somebody? Nobody equals the absence of anyone, the absence of presence and significance, the lack of anyone, the nonappearance or non-presence of a person.

And what do nobodies do? What do they say? What do they think? Why, nothing...nothing at all. Like doormats, which exist to be used, a nobody functions only in ways a somebody thinks appropriate.

Surely everyone must think, say, feel, and do something, but without the essential element of choice, a nobody merely parrots those around them. Original ideas, inventiveness, spontaneity, and raw emotion do not sit well coming from a nobody.

It's okay in a family if a nobody works, eats, and dwells in the home, but never should they have or share an imaginative or original thought. In essence, a nobody, without dreams or hopes of their own, is allowed only an unauthentic life.

Being somebody, that's what our Creator has in mind for us. Somebodies share opinions, ruffle feathers, cause trouble, and sometimes make enemies. Jesus gave us a good example, leaving no doubt that being a somebody amounts to hard work and pain.

We may find we have more relationship challenges with age. Maybe we've allowed our Creator the freedom to move us further from the "nobody-land" of our upbringing to "somebodyville," and some people don't like the change.

If we want no challenges, few ripples in our pond, a shallow life of supposed peace, inner longing, and soul hunger, being a somebody won't suffice. Stepping out of the shadows, crossing over, burning our bridges to Nobody-land challenges us beyond our strength, but the alternative—never claiming our personhood—spells insufferable tragedy and waste.

This passage, though fraught with emotional pain, woos us. In today's Gospel reading, Jesus found a nobody—the man with the crippled hand at the beginning of Mark's third chapter. For once, the needy person didn't find Jesus, Jesus found him. He didn't cry out for healing, but the Lord still met his need.

The Rabbi had just met the Pharisees' judgment for pulling off and eating ripe heads of grain in a field on the Sabbath. According to Pharisaical rules, this was sin. Jesus referred them to the Old Testament, where David and his hungry men ate sacred bread off the altar in the presence of the High Priest.

"The Sabbath was made to serve us; we weren't made to serve the Sabbath. The Son of Man is no lackey to the Sabbath. He's in charge!" These are "somebody" words, and they incite anger.

Jesus returned to the meeting place, where He found the man with the crippled hand. Having such a hand is a sad thing. You can try all you want to get that hand to function, but to no avail. It hangs loose at your side and often gets in your way.

Jesus not only found the man, He addressed him. "Stand here where we can see you." An effective teacher makes use of visuals, and the man must have cooperated. He stood there while Jesus spoke to the people. "What kind of action suits the Sabbath best? Doing good or doing evil? Helping people or leaving them helpless?" No one said a word.

He looked them in the eye, one after another, angry now; furious at their hard-nosed religion. He said to the man, "Hold out your hand." He held it out—it was as good as new!

Jesus shows several emotions in this scene. His patient teaching, pulling an example from King David's life for the religious teachers to contemplate, shows His concern for them. His compassion calls the man forth. That turns to fury when He sees the hardness in the Pharisees' eyes.

To them, this man qualifies as a nobody, his suffering

inconsequential. All that matters to them is their rules. And as we enter into the moment, a sickening sensation of revulsion rises. Jesus's anger sputters in our ears; He's a real person, furious with those who bind others by their trivial rules, and this man is a real person with needs and dignity.

How did the Pharisees react? They fell all over themselves getting out of the meeting place, intent on joining forces with Herod to get rid of Jesus. The juxtaposition of their manic departure with the mystified gratitude filling the man who now looks down at two whole hands brings us to tears.

Who is somebody now? And who are the nobodies? Men who could not suffer a miraculous healing because of their petty, persnickety foibles look pretty small. So do people who hold others down so they can maintain control and set restrictions that stifle growth and spontaneity in their own loved ones.

But when we come forth, called by the Spirit of compassion and liberty all God's children were meant to enjoy, we move beyond the tight-fisted, hard-headed, killing frost of those stipulations. We may suffer people's insecure reactions to so drastic a change, but we wouldn't sacrifice the reclamation of our personhood for anything.

A Nobody on a Mission

Fat little robin, just as cute as all the rest, you peered up at me this morning in an alley. Usually I stop for nothing, so as to get the full benefit of a prolonged walk, and because plenty of renovating awaits me. But today, for you, I stopped. At first I didn't notice that you hopped around on one leg.

One spindly little leg. It's always amazed me what birds can do on their two wiry appendages, but you managed on one. If I hadn't slowed down, I might have missed your condition.

Only one leg supported your bright orange breast and dark feathered back. You went on alert as soon as I stopped to stare at you, fluttered a bit, hopped faster. I ventured a conversation.

"Hi, buddy. Hey, you're doing your work with just one leg, aren't you?"

You stuck to your task, hopping double-time over to a night crawler washed up on the gravel by last night's heavy rain. You grabbed it in your bill and flew to the Smiths' garden to wait for me to leave. Then, I'll bet you forgot all about me.

But I didn't forget you. Three hours later, when I needed a break, I filled a page of my journal with thoughts about you. All day long I kept thinking about your everyday courage to keep providing food for your spouse and babies. They're about the age for flying lessons. I picture you fluffing out with pride as you teach them and observe their first attempts.

You seemed so cool and collected this morning, going about your work as always. I wonder if you've forgotten there's a pretty significant portion of your body missing? You've coped and thrived, survival terms we humans use to describe healing.

So you have healed from whatever misfortune robbed you of a useful, necessary (we would say) body part. Your leg didn't magically reappear and begin functioning—yours wasn't that kind of healing. You somehow learned to get along with one leg.

I wish you could tell me how you lost it. Did a prowling cat rip it from you, did you get caught in a fence, or have you dealt with this defect from birth?

Whatever the circumstances, you adjusted to the situation, accepted reality, and moved on. You aren't whole, some would say, but in a way your wholeness stands out from all other robins. You may be stronger than most, due to your loss. At any rate, you stand here, now, providing for your family, living purposefully in this moment. Bravo!

Today I consider Paul's description of individuals who carry the light of Christ to others in 2 Corinthians 4 (MSG).

> "Remember, our Message is not about ourselves; we're proclaiming Jesus Christ, the Master. All we are is messengers, errand-runners from Jesus for you. It started when God said, 'Light up the darkness!' and our lives filled up with light as we saw and understood God in the face of Christ, all bright and beautiful.
>
> If you only look at *us*, you might well miss the brightness. We carry this precious Message around in the unadorned clay pots of our ordinary lives. That's to prevent anyone from confusing God's incomparable power with us. As it is, there's not much chance of that. You know for yourselves that we're not much to look at."

Unadorned clay pots—not much to look at—errand-runners. God chooses to work through and despite our humanness and our wounds. Sometimes when we think we're unusable, when we lose a leg, He decides to speak through us. The mighty Creator of the universe stoops to work through the likes of us.

It's mind-boggling. If He so chooses, our God can reach us through a one-legged robin, or an elderly woman who survived the rough years to thrive and manifest her Lord's nearness.

Wind

This morning a raging wind bears down on this old house. All manner of creaks and whines issue from the roof, from the corners, from the floor. The building has survived plenty of windstorms, but this one causes it to shudder.

I just read about Jesus walking on the water toward the disciples as they quavered at such a wind on the Sea of Galilee. I can relate. I'm home alone, and the heavy piles of shingles on the roof even shift in this gale. The temperature dropped in the night, and gusts of cold air gust across the floor. Should I put on a third pair of socks?

At least I'm in a safe, dry place, but the disciples struggled on tempestuous water, with oars that refused to cooperate. Jesus had climbed a mountain to pray, and terror gripped their hearts. After all they'd learned from the Master, were they to perish now in this storm?

Virginia comes to mind, a hundred years ago in this very house, minus the extra layers of insulation, new roof, and other adjustments of the generations. Back then, wind surely did more than chase itself through the rooms. I imagine it whipping up her long skirts and chilling her backbone.

Perhaps she worked alone on a day like this, at the beginning of a long, bitter winter. Perhaps she rose from bed after all the children left for school, to wander through this structure and to wonder. Maybe she walked upstairs and stared out at the heaving branches as fear not unlike the disciples' caught at her heart.

What were her private fears, her inner haunts? We have no way of knowing, but they paralyzed her. On a day when rolls of wind ravished the countryside like lightning bolts, maybe Virginia didn't struggle to get up after everyone left, after all.

Maybe she had no desire to peruse walls that held her captive.

The chimes hanging from the covered steps on the back of the house rattle out their skimpy tones today as a maniacal scream rounds the corner, and I wonder that in the midst of such an onslaught, song survives. From her bed, did Virginia listen for sounds of normalcy, lunch pails clinking, sounds that told her the world would not end, that her children were safe? Did her husband come home at noon to check on her, the sound of his footsteps easing her anxiety?

Did she turn in her bed and glimpse a ray of sunshine spread across her quilt through the rattling windowpane? Did the everyday vibration of a steam engine approaching the grain elevator reach below the wind's wail and accompany her breathing? Did the unceasing rhythm of her own heartbeat remind her that life still pulsed within?

In her six-month battles with powers stronger than wind, something more terrifying than a storm on Galilee, did she sense a quiet presence? Did Jesus whisper to her, right in the middle of her agony, that she was not alone?

Swirls

Drifts of snow grace our yard, partially covering grass still unseasonably green after summer's lush rains, and grayish-white dust adorns the inside of our house in similar curlicues. We thought a new furnace and vacuumed heat ducts would take care of this problem.

But after four weeks of using the furnace, we realize our erroneous conclusion. The plumber who installed the ductwork says we need to call a "duct doctor" with a dust-sucker capable of cleaning far beyond our vacuum's poor power. This miracle machine devours century-old cloggings with vengeance.

One more expense. After this inner cleansing, though, will these wafty, delicate bits of fluff, the inspiration for cotton candy, disappear? I'm cynical. Their youthful dance toward the center of the room belies belief. A mop works better that a broom in their pursuit, but still, the sprites elude my reach.

Dust swirls have a life of their own, like inner swirls of self-doubt. Lurking in corners since our youth, they color our perceptions, yet because we focus our energies on immediate tasks, we often ignore them. Too exhausted by the end of the day to pay much attention, we will them away. But suddenly they re-appear, often at the worst times.

As years pass and life slows down, providing more leisure to think, the swirls have a propensity for showing up full-force. A dear friend, almost my exact opposite in many ways, falls into the same pit as I do. Thirty years ago, God brought us together, such an unlikely match. But this woman understands like no one else the effect of self-doubt.

We've taken turns pulling each other out of the pit over the years due to self-loathing, shame's hiss, and an overwhelming sense of unworthiness. But we've told each other that we are worthy and loveable. We've held each other up. Our friendship, like a giant, powerful vacuum in a battle with house dust, has made all the difference. Someone hears us. Someone grew up, as it were, in our childhood home.

Advent begins soon. We fragile humans hold to the comfort brought by this season of darkness and possibility, though it boasts the highest suicide rate. Tired hearts encroached by tangible twists of wooly, elusive swirls make a conscious choice to dwell on possibilities.

Darkness and Possibility

One night a few years ago when my daughter called, my eighteen-month-old grandson played near her while she described his doctor's visit. A few weeks earlier, he'd broken his leg.

"Everything's back to normal, except he cries when we put him in the bathtub. He used to love that. We haven't been able to give him a real bath for three and a half weeks, and now he cries every time we try."

"He's forgotten the joy," I said, later realizing that these words also depicted my emotional state. We experienced more than our share of transitions during the past year with my mom's death and my husband's fourteen-month deployment. I sold our house, moved across the country alone, and started a new job. After the deployment, we bought and moved into this house.

The holidays approach, and we won't be able to be with our children. A little thirty-six-inch artificial tree draped with a few lights decorates our living room. Our family tradition of searching out and bringing home a live evergreen fell by the wayside.

Classes ended for the semester, papers were all corrected, and my spirit hovered in a bad place. Was this discontentment and sadness a dark night of the soul? I clung to the moments when the sunshine cheered me, thankful for sight, health, my husband, teaching, and a home.

The other day, an acquaintance wrote about darkness and possibility dwelling together in Advent—darkness and possibility juxtaposed. As my old "pit" friend would say, "What is, is." But what is can change. Somewhere along the Advent journey, I remembered the joy.

Perpetuity

"And this invitation is for perpetuity." Edna, an elderly neighbor I met a few weeks ago, hailed me in the grocery story to invite me to her church's winter luncheon. Not much taller than her shopping cart, face deeply designed with age, her sparkling blue eyes smiled a welcome.

"How have you been? It's been a long time since I've seen you."

"Do you want the long or short story?" The conspiratorial arch of her brows drew me closer. "Actually, now that the election is over, I'm a lot better."

We continued to discuss that dramatic week, closer to traumatic for Edna. Our nation at the vortex of disaster, on Monday of election week she waited for the next day's local election results with a mixture of hope and fear. Her anxiety just wouldn't stop, she said. How relieved she was at the outcome late the next night.

Her heartfelt sincerity touched me, her concern about the values she espoused, her determination to pass them on to her children and grandchildren. Later, I learned that after the previous national election, the outcome so distressed her that she had to be hospitalized. But there in our grocery store aisle conversation, the tenacious glint in her eyes grew during our five-minute chat.

Even one brief, meaningful conversation per day would do wonders to encourage women who live alone. They've survived duress under which many in my generation, including me, would fold. Now they sit alone in small apartments, memories their main companion.

But here stood Edna, aglow with even a small amount of attention. Her casual use of the word *perpetuity* caught my attention. Where have I heard that level of vocabulary in recent months? This woman's perspicacity remains through all the changes in her world. But then, born before the Great Depression, she lived through World War II.

Somewhere I heard, "Self-control determines your life's outcome." Self-control usually connotes power to avoid doing what we ought not do. But I see this quality in every wrinkle on this octogenarian's face. A friend told me about her battles with depression, but she holds on.

She stays active to the point of becoming ill at the results of an election. "The invitation is for the rest of your life." She gives me a wink. "I love to use that word, perpetuity."

Morning Out with the Ladies

In 1961, William F. Buckley, Jr. wrote an indignant essay published by *Esquire* magazine. He asked, "Why don't we complain?" He explored Americans' unwillingness to make a scene, even when a situation calls for change. After discussing the topic with my class, I've become a little more prone to voice an obvious need when no one else seems able or willing.

Today's women's luncheon brought this essay to mind. With a sinus headache threatening, but a positive, determined attitude and an open mind, I walked over to the church to wait by the front door for my hostess. Greeted warmly and ushered into the fellowship hall, we found a place to sit.

The room's temperature was far too high for such a large group of people. I sat for a while talking with the ladies at my table. Then, I thought of Buckley. After the devotions and singing, I went out into the hallway, where other people agreed with me about the heat. The pastor came by, and hearing our suggestion, hurried to turn down the thermostat.

I returned to my seat with high expectations. This outing would pump up my spirits. But listening to the speaker's dramatic voice, overtrained to project, I realized with dismay that no one made a move to turn down the microphone.

Half an hour later, what had been a baby headache developed into a massive one. The speaker read a script, with hand gestures and voice rises thrown in for effect. No one else seemed to notice. Nearly one hundred women gathered in that room, but not a person budged. Self-control: the Scandinavian variety.

Five minutes later, I thought again of Buckley's treatise

on the importance of speaking up, and left my table. In an adjoining room, I shut the door and sat on the stairs in the sunshine to rub my pounding temples. I could still hear the monologue, which continued for another fifteen minutes.

Later, I asked the woman ahead of me in the lunch line if she enjoyed the presentation.

"She was awfully loud." Relieved to find an honest soul, I stayed long enough to eat a few bites, thanked my hostess, and walked home. This afternoon, I asked another attendee the same question.

The woman blinked. "Her voice was so shrill, it was hard to listen to her, plus I didn't agree with her theology."

Two honest women. My focus turned to the speaker's theology. I hadn't agreed with her viewpoint on angels, either. She threw them in with the popular conception. Angels we all were, she insisted. During the question and answer time, someone disagreed.

"Just because I do something nice for someone doesn't make me an angel."

But the self-appointed expert was adamant.

Since when does caring for other people transform any of us into bona fide angels? I, for one, have about as much angel in me as foam rubber has granite. Expensive ceramic angels graced the centers of our tables today, feminine versions—gossamer-winged, delicate, pastel, fairylike.

Angels, mighty and terrible, fight with unseen but real spiritual forces. They stand guard over portions of the world, answer to the very voice of God. These princes created to do the Almighty's bidding don't lend themselves to pastels.

> Saint Michael the Archangel:
>
> Defend us in battle; be our safeguard against the wickedness and snares of the devil. May God rebuke him, we humbly pray. And do you, O prince of the heavenly host, by the power of God, cast into Hell Satan and all the evil spirits who prowl about the world seeking the ruin of souls.

My headache took me out of the room this morning, a disguised blessing. Kind deeds can transform me into an angel? I don't think so.

But the experience still encouraged me, for some odd reason. Burned out by ten years of public speaking, I'd visualized that gift buried, kaput. *Maybe not,* I thought on my walk home. Canned and gesture-perfect my presentations were not, but they definitely weren't piercing.

Ad Hoc

A chart depicting Army Reserve groups sits on my husband's desk. I happened to notice the term *ad hoc* in one of the little squares filled with names of groups. The computer dictionary describes the meaning as "done or set up solely in response to a particular situation or problem and without considering wider issues."

I glanced around. That's an apt description of several projects around here. Oh, we've tried to mind the broad picture, but if anyone looked closely at any number of areas, they would surely think we hadn't.

Ad hoc, used so often on college campuses to precede "committee," also brings to mind someone with whom I'm far too familiar, someone with a pattern of responding to situations without considering wider issues. I get a little weary following in the wake of her spontaneity at times.

People love her impulsive, contagious excitement, but she spends considerable time wiping up messes she makes along the way. You guessed it, I'm the culprit.

Maybe that's why thinking about self-control as the steering apparatus that guides a ship to its destination attracts my attention. Self-control determines the final outcome of my life? This quality (or lack of it) either strengthens my focus or wreaks havoc on goals.

The difference between partially finished projects and an orderly house with at least one task finished by the end of a day is most often due to self-control. This inner ability to chart one's course becomes more difficult in the fuzzy mental realm. Does self-control define the line between maintaining steady emotions and sinking to an all-time low? Does lack of self-control allow a sense of purposelessness to invade your spirit on days when the winter sun refuses to come out and play?

At the Kansas Parish Nurse Conference, I heard Gracia Burnam's story. She and her husband Martin, kidnapped and held hostage for over a year in the Philippines in 2003, provide an example of self-control in action. Under extreme physical duress in an ad hoc situation, they still maintained mental and spiritual direction. Gracia described her husband's iron resolution, but her own strength prevails as she perseveres after losing Martin.

During my husband's year of deployment, people called me strong. A soldier's purposefulness set the stage, with supporting him my obvious task. I took care of the household even as it moved across the nation, kept an eye on our accounts and let him know what was happening.

Self-control came more easily in those ad hoc days. Everything was a reaction to the deployment, yet we decided to move back to the Midwest considering wider issues. But unplanned events evolved. Our grandson threatened to arrive early, and I had no job for several months.

With no set schedule, I could travel to help with the baby. But as I returned and transitioned into the rhythm of normal life, nothing seemed normal. Could "ad hoc" last a lifetime? Now I recall all the good that occurred during that time. God cared for us as we transitioned, transitioned, and transitioned again.

Life is in the interruptions. Ad hoc periods unsettle us, but also provide opportunities to practice self-control.

Naomi

"God has turned on me." Utter desolation tinged Sally's tone.

After a description of her troubled marriage, her daughter's health problems, and recent frightening financial events, this retreat participant's statement rang with logic. She lay in the dust, like Naomi in the Old Testament book of Ruth.

Naomi suffered the loss of her husband, her sons, her homeland—every earthly hope. Bitterness bedded down in her spirit, with Naomi too weary to resist.

This modern-day woman, too, succumbed to despair. When bitterness moves in, despair soon follows, since hope cannot thrive in negativity. As our retreat proceeded, she revealed even more devastating experiences. Would this downward spiral never end?

Worse, was God still in this with her? All outward appearances shouted "No!" Of course, she didn't need a reminder about Naomi. She already knew the biblical story well, but living a story is different from studying it.

The only response worthy of her suffering was a listening ear. No pat answers, as if any existed, anyway. The only comfort the other participants could offer was companionable silence.

More than one issued an invitation as we parted. "If you need to talk again, please give me a call."

Weeks later, I rocked my granddaughter, who'd wakened from her nap in tears. She needed solace, but didn't want to be held, needed more sleep, but couldn't return to that state. Or was that a cry of pain? Teething? An earache? I held her, let her down, then gathered her in my arms again, incapable of providing the perfect antidote.

Just so, God the Father holds that retreat participant, even though relief seems out of reach for her. The parallel breaks down, of course, since God knows precisely what she needs, while I tried every obvious solution for my granddaughter, and hours later, still had no idea what had troubled her.

That evening, in her high chair eating chicken, brown rice, and green beans for dinner, she clapped her chubby hands in toddler joy, as if her every wish were granted. I cupped her sweet, expressive face in my palms and kissed her nose, thinking of Sally.

Had she remembered the joy yet? As evening came to her day, did she clutch a reminder of God's presence? I hope my granddaughter remembered one thing—I remained with her, focused totally on her needs, with no intention of leaving.

Part Five

"'Stay' is a charming word in a friend's vocabulary."
~ Louisa May Alcott

Community of Women

Sometimes we become isolated, even though we know the important role our female friends play. One day in the first months after our move, I sat with an old friend, a newer one, and four other women around a holiday table. My old friend, the one who painted our ceilings, used her intuitive gift of hospitality when she invited me to join this group at the last minute.

Laughter and light from their faces warmed me. The subject of conversation could have been anything, but mostly it centered on connections—how all of us ended up in this particular home at this time. Two of the women lived in the same town years ago and maintained a close relationship through several moves. Two others still live there, and the last two are brand-new friends of one or the other of these original buddies.

One of my students endured a breast biopsy that afternoon. After working in a large insurance office for nineteen years, she decided to go to college. Class ended in one week, so we let down all formality. We planned to start a writing group after the holidays, a great reason for not dreading the end of our class so much.

The next morning I received her e-mail: "BENIGN, BENIGN, BENIGN!" She mentioned how much our class meant to her. Another class member who had also been out in the working world for about the same amount of time echoed her sentiments as we walked to our cars the last night after class.

Someday, I thought, *I'll let them know how reading their writings and facilitating their response groups helped me through a tough season.*

Cold December sweeps in, and cloudy days thwart our efforts to maintain cheer. Women need one another. Did friendship elude Virginia at the turn of the century, with her busy household?

Through long, harsh winters on the farm, did Grace and my mother crave the companionship of other women? I think so. While Lance and I spent months in a developing country, remoteness from like-minded people created the toughest obstacle. Distance from others thrills some solo adventurers, but for us, friends could have made the difference.

Scriptural friendships abound—David and Jonathan, Jesus and John the Baptist, the ardent souls who lowered their friend through a roof for healing. That man might have spent his entire life on his stretcher apart from their kindness and concern.

More than one comatose patient has returned to this world at the urging of a loved one's voice. There's nothing like that understanding whisper, nothing like a friend's wooing to strum us back from the edge of the pit.

Human Gifts

What we need comes to us, although we don't always recognize our name on the package. For a friend of mine named Kin, one of the joys of working in a small gift/espresso shop was anticipating who might walk through the door.

A customer described her favorite wine. "Made from grapes of two colors, the fizz rises from the interaction of the two." Hmm. A young woman traversing difficult roads in a relationship stood nearby and heard the comment. After the customer left, she confessed to my friend the gift she received—two extremely different personalities can mingle together with eventual pleasant results.

On that particular day, someone's knowledge of the chemical workings of wine provided the exact blend of comfort and encouragement she sought. Tears of resolve flooded her eyes. Maybe there was still hope. The giver had no idea what she gave.

Another time, a snarly customer obviously having a bad day brought another sort of present for Kin to unwrap. Her demanding tone required compliance, but what she asked was too much.

Still she supplied my friend with an opportunity to practice a fledgling skill, saying no. Of course, the customer had no clue about Kin's lifelong effort to speak that rascal two-letter word without guilt. But as the woman exited the shop, flustered and not a little angry, Kin straightened her shoulders. Just because the customer knew how to intimidate didn't mean Kin couldn't stand up for what she knew was right.

Gifts, obvious and hidden, dressed in negative or positive clothes, abound as we interact with people. Sometimes they hearten us for our journeys, sometimes they offer us scenarios in which to play new roles and find fresh victories.

Immigrant

The winter I lived alone during Lance's deployment, my hiatus from our normal Sunday regimen freed me to visit various churches (or not), and the adventure brightened long weekends. The most "different"—a Greek Orthodox church not far from where I lived—intrigued me. Its ornate sanctuary and long-robed priest brought back the beauty and mystery of one Christmas Eve mass to which Mom and our neighbor lady, in a spurt of ecumenism, took me during adolescence. Then, rich words poured forth in Latin. This time, I attempted to follow along in Greek.

Meeting new people went along with these experiences, or I had the exotic luxury of remaining anonymous. I usually chose the latter. Anonymity in a worship setting has always appealed to me for some reason. At the Catholic church in our town, I would slip into a back pew with the parents of squirming young children and soak in the artwork of windows, architecture, and liturgy wafting to me over the long rows of shined mahogany pews.

Once, on the front steps, I met a vibrant young Vietnamese-American woman herding her eighteen-month-old son. She sought help her with her writing, and I'd longed to find unique venues for my English-as-a-second-language teaching skills. We were meant to meet.

The next week, we waged battle against the English language. Jenna's logical questions brought out the best in me. I love to explain seemingly illogical grammatical concepts. What example could I share to clarify a gnarly linguistic tangle that had bothered this sharp young woman her entire life?

For many individuals, becoming bilingual qualifies as a life-long process, unless they begin their use and study of the second language at a very young age, with plenty of chances to speak and write. No one could possibly have worked harder at understanding the nuances of our tongue than Jenna, but complicated human expressions can withhold their mysteries. This young mother and wife grappled with concepts linguists analyze for entire lifetimes.

I wanted to convey to Jenna what she brings to native English speakers. Her essays give insights from another way of seeing life, glimpses impossible for me to conjure. We grew to adulthood separated by a world, a generation, and a terrible war. If only she could realize the cultural gift she bears, and if only our society could, too.

She asked if her language challenges resembled those of other students. The answer, of course, was "absolutely." Any difference lay in her tenacity to probe the conundrums of English grammar. She wanted a formula, some definitive answer for each grammatical and semantic query that would ensure success in understanding our complex language.

She and I have much in common—a hunger to learn, a thirst to succeed, a desire to arrive. As her instructor, problem solving brought challenge and satisfaction, but for Jenna, frustration sometimes reigned. Describing her task as arduous, and more of a *being* than a *doing* did not suffice. Grammar cannot magically take root in one's mind—the process involves practice, making mistakes, and relinquishing our ideas of perfection.

I understood her dissatisfaction with this kind of encouragement. It's what I've faced my whole spiritual life. How can we accept life as a series of situations provided for us to develop conquering grace? We know it's true, but we don't want to hear it. We want to *arrive*.

Accepting the lack of answers would smooth our way, but our humanness prevents such acquiescence. Words by Maltbie D. Babcock—written in 1901 and still with me from my eighth grade memorize-a-poem-a-week year—remind us that life and struggle are synonymous:

Be strong!

We are not here to play, to dream, to drift;
We have hard work to do and loads to lift;
Shun not the struggle, face it, 'tis God's gift.
Be strong, be strong, be strong!

The Science of Language

My Introduction to Linguistics class members submit their linguistic autobiographies. The project helps them discover the incredible power of their own histories. From infant's cry to feebler adult wails, what would we do without our voices? Part of our purpose on earth is to speak our messages. When shame or fear silence us, the loss is incalculable.

Even without words, meaning exists in our birthing cries. There's no end to studying how the miracle of speech occurs. Our words extend from Mom to world, defining experience. At two, my granddaughter has mastered so much of English grammar I stand in awe. She verbalizes even complex sentences, using pronouns, tense, and vocabulary with alacrity.

Soon she and her brother will learn to read...he already prints his name. They will use symbols to express reality, and then before I know it, they'll move out into the wide world, their power with words one of their greatest gifts.

On days when we quail under the work we have to do, the gloomy weather, discouraging circumstances or a relationship gone awry, we can call to mind our ability to communicate. If we enjoy this ability, we can give thanks. We have only to meet people who have lost this gift to renew our wonder.

Every time we listen, we encourage others to voice their perceptions. Every time we build someone up whose voice has succumbed to a shame-based system, we inspire hope. Only a toxic parent rejects the beauty of their child's voice, the expression of their personhood, and it may not be too late to motivate the telling of a unique story.

Rooms

Women of age are treasure troves. Their determined individualism offers lessons about love, hate, tenacity, integrity, bitterness, survival, honesty's reward, and grace. Mostly I listen in the presence of these wellsprings of life, watch and listen.

The tip of their heads, the far-away look as they reminisce a particularly painful episode, the contagion of their laughter when caught in a moment of delight, the quiet of their spirits at certain memories—all of these exhibit quality of character and garnered wisdom.

During this cold season, I check on a geranium wintering over and discover all is well. I count ten potential bright blossoms. Women of age winter over too. They hunker down with creative projects. The other day my neighbor re-taught me to crochet, because the curtains for an upstairs window need some kind of hooks. I say re-taught because I learned to crochet once while convalescing from surgery.

Last week, though, when I picked up a hook, my fingers didn't recall what to do, so my neighbor, who taught her own children to crochet, guided me back into productivity. A month ago, unmotivated to paint and make decisions about furniture and windows, I ignored the piles of boxes still crowding that little room at the top of the stairs, but now I'm ready. I will claim this corner, too.

The same process repeats itself with my inner life. In the same way I've walked by that room hundreds of times on my way to the computer, I skirt closed inner doors. Avoidance works for a while.

Sometimes there's wisdom in pretending a certain room doesn't exist. Maybe we honestly don't have the strength today to face the piled boxes, walls begging to be cleaned and painted, cupboards needing to be organized. At times, walking right on by might be the most efficient choice we can make. The room, we know, will always exist, because rooms don't go away.

As long as we deal with them sometime, instead of denying their reality, hope remains. But if we move into total denial, the spaces keep filling up until we have no idea what waits in the disarray, dust takes over, and the room's existence becomes a problem.

Rooms of unaddressed anger and hurt will not remain covert forever. Truth requires disclosure. If ignored, truth pops out when we least expect it. A solid, faithful, generous woman from one of the places I've lived lashes out at her husband for no apparent reason. Harshness laces her voice. Against her will, a door has opened to one of those neglected rooms in her spirit. Her expression declares her wish to take back the words and the attitude so foreign to the usually kind face she shows the world.

She believes in and has tried to live out scriptural obedience to her husband, but at odd moments, caught unawares, he reels at the sound of her sharp reprimand. He skulks away on tenuous feet, a little boy shamed and hurting. A simple miscalculation he made in an undertaking the couple had attempted together set in motion such vehemence. Do her cutting remarks signal retribution for slights put on mental shelves in years past?

Perhaps this bitter tone which surfaces unbidden in her later years originates in a room she's walked by for decades, stalwart in her determination to keep the rest of the house, the part people see, tidy and presentable. Perhaps the origin of this voice lies buried under too much emotional debris to uncover. After all these years, the possibility of revealing its source looms too dreadful for her to consider.

So this harshness continues to slide out of hiding at the most inconvenient times. All manner of rooms, as long as we live, will always await our attention. Like the one at the top of the stairs that so needs my ministrations, rooms simply don't go away.

Deep Healing

In the Midwest in the middle of winter, catching a nasty head cold is no big surprise, and I'm grateful to be spared the throbbing pain that normally occurs behind my eyes. In the wee hours, I hit the couch and checked out the inspirational network. First I found a healer man, Elmer Gantry style. One of his facial expressions when he prayed made me wonder if something was stuck in his nasal cavity, too.

The crowd was in a fervor, and people gathered around various folks seeking healing. Then, the spotlights zoomed in as one lady rose from her wheelchair. Her obesity made it even tougher to believe she would walk.

Every section of her body was huge, and it all slid downward. She walked with a man on either arm, then shook them off and walked all by herself. Wow. But nothing about this service reminded me of Jesus healing the man with the crippled hand. The pastor ran around the stage wiping perspiration from his face, his head thrown back, a coarse whisper emanating from his lips, "Jesus...Jesus...Jesus...Jesus!"

I turned the dial to a Jewish-Christian service. A rabbi wearing a *kippah* and all the other priestly garments stood behind a pulpit. No shiny designer suit, tie, and shirt for him. He gazed into the camera, his eyes warm above a dark beard, to offer listeners hope through the magnanimous promises in Ephesians and Colossians.

"Sure, I pray like everyone else, for a cabin beside a flowing stream, a new car, but some things I know for *sure* God wants us to enjoy." Then he read wondrous, flowing poetic language about our spirits being strengthened, that we may know Christ, the fullness of God, that we may experience the depth and breadth and height of God's mighty love.

His prayers, uttered quietly in melodic King James Version, sustained my soul. These requests, he said, we pray with absolute certainty, as our spiritual growth is, without doubt, the Father's will.

What a contrast. And, thanks to technology, we can tune in to the gamut of worship styles, from religious fever pitch to self-control and utter Word-centeredness. When the rabbi intoned the prayers for our spirits to grow, I joined him. That, I know for sure I need, and his invoking God's strength upon us also seemed appropriate for sons and daughters in war zones and people in grief.

I can't help ruminating on the differences between those two services. Each of them appeals to certain people, and God allows for great divergence among His children. All our babbling rises, like incense, toward heaven. He waits to hear our voices, waits to bless us.

In the first service, I leaned my heavy head against the back of our couch. "Yes, please heal me." At the same time, I recognized that my greatest need today is to be quiet, to pray for someone far away who digests terrible news. Would I be doing that without the cold? Chances are, I'd be running around, catching up on a million unfinished projects.

In the second, my love of English literature and the deep desires of my heart took over. The Almighty God desires that we fathom the full dimension of His love. What could be sweeter? As the day passes, I contemplate the wide world God sets before us, and I think my word for today is *prayer*.

Mother of Mary

On December eleventh, Advent highlights Mary's mother. We don't know her name, and few details exist concerning her role in the outrageous drama of our Savior's birth. A common peasant woman married to a citizen of Nazareth, a small Galilean town, her simplicity baffles us.

How did she feel when her daughter suddenly decided to visit her cousin Elizabeth in the hill country of Judah? Had Mary described the angel Gabriel's appearance, complete with the astounding message that she would soon become pregnant with a holy child? What was her response to the news of Elizabeth's miracle pregnancy at such an advanced age?

What did Mary's mother do with all the wild goings-on in her life? Was Elizabeth related on the maternal or paternal side? How did Mary's mother and father spend those three months while their daughter stayed with this cousin? Probably they went about their business, but their thought lives must have overflowed with anxiety.

Mary probably stayed with Elizabeth for baby John's birth. Did Mary's mom entertain jealous feelings as Elizabeth became her daughter's mentor? The Scriptures leave this question open. We know that Joseph discovered Mary's condition before the consummation of the marriage and that God guided him through a dream to accept his betrothed "as is."

But what about Mary's mother? To be pregnant out of wedlock involved such cultural shame that Mary could have faced death by stoning. The well-laid plans Mary's mother had for her daughter's life had gone astray.

Talk about accepting unacceptable circumstances. We

imagine this mother's face as her young daughter divulges the angel's secret, or as Joseph shares God's night message. Furrows deepen in her brow, her jaw sets, she holds her breath for full minutes, and then sighs from a painful cavity far in the recesses of her being.

Her daughter, always trustworthy before, and this man Joseph, whom the family had known as honorable since his birth. Surely they would not lie to her face? Yet, human conception occurred in only one way. Did this woman wrack her brain, imagining times Joseph and Mary might have slipped away together?

We see her shaking her head as she considers Mary's explanation. No, this is not possible. Mary, who swore she had known no man, had always been committed to purity, and Joseph vowed before Jehovah that he had not violated her daughter. Then how could she be with child? Speechless with shock, did this mother lash out in alarm and anger, or contain her outrage until later, in an outburst with her husband?

Did tears start as the two spoke or wait until she lay alone on her bed in sleepless nights to follow? Did her husband comfort her? To what woman friend could she possibly pour out this incredible, unbelievable tale? In a dream, did an angel appear to guide Mary's mother, too? Did she visit Elizabeth with her daughter, to see with her own eyes another mighty God-work, and thus receive sustenance to absorb reality?

Or was her cache of "older women" confined to those she knew from ancient stories engraved in her consciousness from youth? Did she find comradeship with Sarah, who laughed at the prediction that she'd bear a child in her old age, or with Esther, whom the Almighty used to do the impossible in Babylon during the reign of King Xerxes?

Did Mary's mother experience the "communion of saints" in the way my Egyptian seatmate described? Was Mary her first child? Did she sense her own mother cheering her on? We don't know, but Mary came back from visiting Elizabeth; did she ever live under her parents' roof again?

What engaged Mary's mother on the day Joseph took her

daughter, now his extremely expectant wife, to report for the census? Did she accompany her own husband to Jerusalem? Either way, questions must have swarmed through her mind. When would she get to see the baby? Who would help Mary with the birth?

The New Testament leaves us to wonder. After presenting the infant in Jerusalem, one Gospel tells us the little family returned to Nazareth. How long did they stay there? This story contains enough of an outline, without ever mentioning Mary's mother, to create in the reader a well of compassion for this new grandmother.

Family relationships provide some of our greatest human joys but can also cause intense sorrow. Consider Mary's mother while Joseph moves Mary and their son to Egypt in response to an angel's instructions. How could she not entertain grave doubts about this impetuous move? Did she know about God's provision for their needs through the wise men's gifts?

The Bible tells us that Joseph again obeyed God's angel in a dream, taking Mary and Jesus under cover of darkness on what must have seemed a strange and foolhardy journey. Did he inform Mary's parents before they departed, or were they left to wonder where their daughter and grandchild went?

Either way, that night and the next day surely brought consternation. What kind of man would leave everything behind to set out on a long, dangerous trek with a wife and child in the middle of the night? Forced to accept an untenable situation a second time, what choice did Mary's parents have? Her father could have torn out in a wild chase to find the little family. Maybe he did. Most likely, Mary's mother grieved in silence.

Did they receive any news from Joseph and Mary during their Egyptian sojourn? Presumably not, since secrecy was essential to Jesus's safety. In the sleepless early morning hours, did this mother and grandmother wonder where she had gone wrong as she recited the events of the past months?

Did she visit the house where Joseph and Mary brought Jesus, his first home after his presentation at the temple in Jerusalem, to stand where they had so recently slept, to visualize their flight and to wonder? Did she pick up a scrap of cloth to hold close for comfort, a small blanket they left in their haste?

And in the following months, sometimes at mid-morning, did she wander over to that place again, hoping against hope they might have returned, that this entire ordeal was a nasty nightmare? Pausing as she washed the clothes, did she look up, gaze off into the distance, and imagine them coming back along the road? How many prayers rose from her heart for her loved ones?

Left with empty arms, she lost the possibility of rejoicing in this baby's growth. Grandparents hurt. In all kinds of scenarios as their adult children forge and reforge their lives, grandparents hurt.

After Herod's death, when they could safely return to Israel, Joseph once again obeyed an angel's command. He re-entered his homeland and decided exactly where to end their travels. A final dream—as far as we know—pointed him to the Galilean hills, to a village called Nazareth.

Now, Mary's mother celebrates their arrival. She would be able to know this grandson and have some input in his life. They would enjoy family dinners and she would have long talks with her daughter. The deliciousness takes us beyond words, one mother's comfort complete.

Gleanings

During our African sojourn, a Norwegian missionary needed a place to stay for a few days and joined us at our mission station. She brightened our lives at a critical time. She could not have known how much we needed a grandma.

From this tall, slender, white-haired woman I learned to make Norwegian pancakes filled with fruit and yogurt. Our family has enjoyed these delicacies for many years. She also helped me design and sew extra diapers because the strong desert sun and wind soon ravaged our supply.

In her unassuming, soft-voiced way, Anna taught us my favorite table grace.

> Thank You for the world so sweet,
> Thank You for the food we eat.
> Thank You for the birds that sing,
> Thank You, Lord, for everything.
> Amen

Our children, one and a half and three at the time, loved Anna. She encouraged me in practical ways when I most needed help, and her mealtime prayer is one we still use. The last line of her heartfelt melody bears repeating. "Thank You, Lord, for everything."

Chatting

A fierce fifty-plus-mile-an-hour wind batters the house. Unless ice covers the streets, I rarely miss my walk, but today my sinuses hold up a red stop sign. Unless I want them to throb even more, this is one walk to skip.

A week before Christmas, we entertained some friends. Mara saw our "new" house in August just before we made the purchase. She visualized possibilities. When they joined us for dinner, she reminded us how far the work had come. Her husband hadn't seen the house, and expected the worst after hearing her dire descriptions.

She declared, "I just can't believe they're buying that house! I don't know if I could handle a renovation like that." Probably it's a good thing she kept those thoughts to herself, because they still fit my sentiments. When they came for dinner, Christmas decorations helped the effect. A few baskets of velvety dark red poinsettias, candles, and our tiny, lighted tree helped to hide incessant flaws.

Candlelight softened faces as well as surroundings while we caught up on the past four months. The men remained at the dining room table, while Mara and I plopped in the Christmas tree corner. We explored her teaching escapades, our grown children's adventures, and our recent "lessons from heaven."

Although distance and busyness separated us for a time, we picked up right where we left off, and hearing the buzz of our husbands chatting heartened us. Recent studies cite that isolation stalks men, especially in midlife.

My father-in-law called chatting "gossiping," a statement his wife of nearly sixty years responded to with laughter. She had waited too many times for him to conclude a conversation.

Women today have nearly everything we need in our own

homes, and many of us lack energy to socialize. We even have difficulty finding opportunities to talk with our children. As I washed dishes with friends after a meal the other day, one of the older women said, "I think kids these days miss out on washing dishes with their moms. We used to talk things over every evening."

I can identify. In Dad's large extended family, the privilege of helping with dishes was one "coming of age" sign. Stationed at the sink, I knew I belonged.

In fact, this is my clearest memory of holidays—hard at work scrubbing silverware, plates, and glasses. Inevitably, Uncle Jim sauntered up behind us, cup in hand, saying he just had to have a drink of water. Would we mind?

Well, yes, we would. By the time he cooled the water by running it into the dishpan, our dishwater would be tepid. But he never failed us. Aware of this particular uncle's idiosyncrasies, we sighed, shrugged our shoulders, and reheated the water. I remember feeling like one of the women the first time he sidled behind my Aunt and me.

"Excuse me, please."

Sharing in that generational cleanup process mellowed us after the meal. The same was true for Mara and me, sitting in the corner and sharing another kind of "comfort food." A simple evening at home with old friends gives us perspective. Although we did nothing more than eat and talk, we found new strength. Chatting is not wasted time.

Part Six

Starshine

In a little stall in a stable bare,
so suddenly the Lord was there.
Such cramped quarters, dingy and dark,
an unlikely place, smelly and stark.

Stars shone bright over that small town,
and the angels sang as Christ came down.
They all worshipped Him, and we worship too.
He came to earth for me, for you.

John the Baptist

No Advent season would be complete without John the Baptist's role in the story. If John lived today, he might be diagnosed with adult ADHD and immediately medicated. He exuded such confidence in his role of readying people for the Savior. Elizabeth and Zechariah prepared him well to make do in the wilderness and use the voice God gave him.

John spoke with authority to the most powerful leaders in his community. "Bigger than life," he blazed his way through political, religious, and cultural taboos without wincing. Thrown into prison on a whim by a drunken, lustful ruler to satisfy a self-centered, vicious woman, he languished with no crowds to address, no keen wilderness air to breathe, no hills to climb, and no hope of release.

Awaiting certain death, he sent his followers to ask Christ if He was really the Messiah. Oh, in his head John knew. He entertained no doubts about Jesus's divinity when the dove descended and divine words identified Jesus as the Chosen One.

But there in the dark, dank, lonely prison with far too much time to think, his mind clouded. Places and circumstances can send frail humans into a downward spiral, as happened to us in the Sahel. John started to think too much and doubted himself. What if he hadn't yet fulfilled his life's purpose? What if somehow he had missed out on his destiny? What if, by some horrible accident, he had gotten it all wrong?

Fraught with anxiety, this courageous, assertive man went straight to the source for answers. The response his friends carried back from Jesus endowed him with strength to endure a gruesome, ignominious death. True, God did not spare him an undignified end, for he kept company with the prophets of old. But he could leave this world at peace.

The first time I heard a speaker describe John's depression, I, too, took heart.

> "Just because you're down, with morose thoughts haunting you, doesn't mean hope is lost. The Lord took time to outline his answer to John's friends, quoting from a passage in Isaiah 35 familiar to John since his youth. Jesus gave his doubting cousin definite examples to prove His identity."

John's slip into doubt changed nothing about his relationship with Jesus. We don't hear the Messiah, arms akimbo, bluster at the Baptist's questions. In addition to giving the evidence John needed, the Lord's personal answer also included an empowering benediction: "Blessed is the man who does not fall away on account of me" (Matthew 11, NIV).

John needed a word from God. No doubt, he knew how to meditate on Scripture, but in his weakness, he craved a special word. With Jesus's final message, he could persevere. He had fulfilled his mission. Jesus's message overwhelmed him with a sense of God's love.

Maybe he castigated himself for giving in to negative thinking, but still, he must have breathed an enormous sigh of relief and, at peace again, slept well that night. Maybe the Spirit gave him one word to ponder, as we do in Lectio Divina, until the soldiers came for his head. Perhaps it was "blessed," perhaps it was "not." No, he would not fall away.

His circumstances hadn't changed, but he embraced his personal power anew. Never again would he stride fearlessly through the wilderness, but he experienced inner victory that no one could take away. Having dipped into mental and emotional weakness, he could face death with strength.

Like Grace's message from her friend Marcia, Jesus's communiqué lightened John's heart and renewed his faith. In the same way, words become our sustenance, often through the mouths of friends.

Good News

Julian of Norwich lived in the fourteenth century. She prayed for three gifts from God—to visualize Christ's suffering and death as if she had witnessed them, a deathly sickness, and three wounds. She asked for contrition, compassion, and a total longing for God.

At thirty, her prayers became reality as she lay close to death for seven days and experienced sixteen revelations of Christ's crucifixion. For the next two decades, she deciphered the visions' meaning.

Julian lived in a solitary room with a window into the Norwich sanctuary so she could participate in worship services. Her room's other window allowed her to counsel people seeking advice and prayers. Separated from the daily life of her times, which included plagues and wars, she still influenced her world.

Christ's messages to her intrigue us, especially her absolute assurance of God's enduring love for humanity, a love that ultimately triumphs over evil. "All shall be well," this holy woman repeatedly quoted her Lord.

Julian believed God's image composes our substance. Thus God could say, "It is good," as He completed creation. But as sensual beings we can ignore God, making our created state an end in itself. To Julian, sin is that which creates mental agony, self-blame, shame, and physical suffering.

We forget that we come from God, become self-absorbed with our own distress, and forget God's continuing love. Our negative emotions focus on divine anger, and we think God blam[illegible]s us for our fall. According to Julian, our Creator [illegible] His wish for our good through the incarnation, when [illegible] on our sorrows to unite us with God and with our

Human freedom allows us choice so we can experience the meaning of separation from God. Meanwhile, God's constant love keeps us in life, even when we don't acknowledge His care. Through Christ's vicarious suffering, God draws us back to Himself. In eternity, we will know the absence of all sorrow and loss.

We consistently bear the image of God. Julian believed we never lose that divine image, as Jesus did when He bore the world's sin. God never forgets who we are, even if we do. Our sin, though despicable, does not define us. In the end, all will be well.

How? We cannot fully know, but our faith foretells our transformation, although we may not comprehend the process. Our lives always matter to God. I breathe deeply as I think about Julian. One sacred phrase surfaces: unconditional acceptance. It wiggles through my consciousness like balm.

Julian's concept of Christianity differs greatly from what I used to believe. The missing element? Condemnation. I learned that God turns His face from us as filthy rags without one iota of goodness or worth. We do not merit repair. Rather than revealing the inestimable value of union with our Creator, sin makes us so utterly disgusting that He turns His eyes away from such a sickening sight.

Julian attributes no such mercilessness to God. She sees humans, even before redemption, as beloved children with continual worth. Christ, then, exemplifies the fullness of the Father's love for us.

The difference in these teachings lies in God's attitude toward us during our time of separation. Does He keep His distance, pick up His coattails so they don't contact us, and hold His nose as He walks by? Or does He still love us as prodigals, even before our redemption? Does He long and wait for us to start the journey home, as did the father of the prodigal son?

Separated as we were by an innate sense of shame, did God ever stop loving us? Did the Good News shock us into fear and trembling, play on the terror of punishment and on our low self-concept, like a metal sign jutting from a lawn on a hazy morning walk? Or did the message meet our underlying need for acceptance?

Surrounded with testimonies of deliverance from drug abuse, sexual promiscuity, and the "anything goes" philosophy, I greeted the Gospel with a sense of absolute unworthiness and amazement. Although my story included no "big sins," believing God could ever look on me with favor seemed impossible.

It would take years to comprehend that perhaps my greatest trespass lay in being afraid to live, unable to do anything for fear of punishment, my walls of shame as formidable as any built by honest sin. My entire psyche revolved around two words—fear and punishment.

Julian's portrait of an unchanging God holds intrinsic comfort. Reborn and fed through Christ's body, we imagine ourselves (yes, even our Protestant selves), held in the same never-ending compassion we extend toward our own children and grandchildren. Embraced from birth, how can our offspring enjoy deeper love than what our Heavenly Father offers us? This move from trembling to rejoicing takes some time.

Coming of Age

At the beginning of John's fourteenth chapter, Jesus tells the disciples not to let their "hearts be troubled." When I memorized this verse in the King James Version, I understood *troubled*. Troubled described my heart much of the time. That inner dis-ease led to lack of confidence, fear, and self-doubt. I memorized this and other verses in hopes that my faith would grow, but confidence didn't come easily or quickly.

In our family, one sign you'd almost arrived at adulthood—or at least that the adults hoped you might someday—was getting to play 500. We hung around the card table as our grandparents played our parents, or the men played the women, or friends played friends, longing for the day when we would be considered sagacious enough to fill one of the chairs. We planned how we would handle the responsibilities of arranging the cards in our right hand, deciding what to bid, actually bidding, and then "taking tricks."

For a while, some of our relatives played Canasta, and then Kings in the Corner, but 500 remained *the* game. When aunts and uncles came for our birthdays, the game turned serious. Once, Grandma and her sister Evie partnered. They enjoyed quite the winning streak until their foes realized they passed cards under the table between their toes.

Grandma, my heroine, my mainstay! I could scarcely believe she had cheated, but she had, and everyone laughed. In my black and white world, a puzzle piece refused to fit, so I chalked this blooper up to Aunt Evie's presence. She had an even wider, flatter nose than Grandma, and people called her "a character." The cheating was her idea, and Grandma went along with her to avoid hurting her feelings.

Years passed. Watching and watching, game after game,

evening after evening, we began to feel we could manage taking an adult spot and started begging. Finally, one evening when Dad sat at another table, Mom relented.

I remember nothing about the game except making it through. Akin to helping with the dishes after holiday dinners, this peculiar bar mitzvah catapulted my brother and me into acceptance. Maybe I got into the circle a little younger than he, but by then, Mom, with two younger children under foot, had little energy for keeping track.

From that time on, we played whenever we had the chance. Not long after our marriage, my husband and I played 500 one night with his parents. His dad bid high and didn't mess around.

I discovered that bidding three, a huge risk for me, couldn't win the bid away from a born risk-taker who *liked* bidding. His self-confidence prevented him from suffering if he and his partner lost, the exact opposite of my reaction. My fear of failure or losing my partner's approval if we lost a bid led to wasting some classic hands.

It's been years since we've played 500, and if we ever start, I may be a more forceful bidder than when my father-in-law smoked us. A great deal more of Grandma lives in me now, and of Julian of Norwich. The possibility of failure wouldn't bother me half as much, and I'd have a whole lot more fun. Confidence and an untroubled heart make a big difference, even in seemingly trivial areas of our lives.

Little Green Room

The shade of green somewhere between what used to be called olive and what used to be called lime will never again cover our walls. We have now lived in four homes, and in each one, this color of green dominated at the outset.

The entire outside of one house bore this hue, but it had the front porch I desired. Lance hated the color, so during his two-week Army Reserve training, several friends and I transformed every square inch to white. One couple sacrificed an entire Saturday, and another man crawled like a cat into crevices under the roof one morning at six a.m.

Of course, the house we're working on now came clothed in our favorite green. The living room, dining room, and an upstairs bedroom displayed the exact shade Lance calls Army Puke Green, or APG. Living in military housing as a youth, he saw far more of this than any other color, so he has had enough. I don't recall how rooms were painted in my first childhood home; color didn't matter.

But the hue of our upstairs room decorated my elementary school. They ought to label cans containing this substance "chemical green," because it's unnatural. When it covers entire walls, the result hurts the eyes.

Surely no one would choose to wrap their world in APG. Maybe most of this paint came into use after World War II, when only a few colors were available? I don't know, but my motivation runs high to eradicate every trace on the walls of our small upstairs bedroom.

When we first bought the house, I envisioned this room as the grandchildren's space. Buried in downstairs renovations, I lost sight of that goal, but when fall semester ended, my ambition returned. By mid-morning the first day, I cleared out one corner crowded with boxes. A pile at the top of the stairs waited for transfer to the garage, another to the basement, and another to the garbage.

Those windows had stayed shut for years. Layers of peeling paint lined the casements, so I chipped away at them and took aim with the Shop Vac. Scraps flew like insects onto the carpet, highlighting the real dead insects that met their demise in the cracks between storm window and casement.

I gazed at piles of orange and black "lady bugs" imported from Japan to eat a certain moth that infests soybean fields. Now the imports plague us in spring until the soybeans mature, and again in fall until the first hard frost. Downstairs, I snuffed out massive numbers. Discovering new ways to remove them from ceiling corners became a kind of game.

These little creatures stink, and leave a black, suspect trail on walls and curtains. In the midst of our frustrations with this old house, daily victories over these pests came close to being fun. I have to say, though, that they provide a picture of tenacity and perseverance. Just when you think the weather's frigid enough, and surely you've vacuumed up every last one, you hear a familiar "crunch" under your shoe.

A former ESL student, a gentle young Buddhist woman from Thailand, would have a fit watching me search and destroy. She objected when I brandished the flyswatter to rid our study area of pesky flies.

Tackling that little room upstairs brought two-fold joy. I found some items I'd forgotten, and the job showed rapid progress. Best of all, a cheery yellow covered APG.

The Colors of Life

On gloomy days I walk into our yellow room for fun, just to be cheered. I once preferred red, the power color, but in those days, meaning never entered my decisions. I had no idea meanings could be assigned to colors. When I do something, I do it "whole-hog," as they say in the Midwest. So red was always my first pick, regardless of the options.

Brown-eyed people ought not to wear blue, I believed, as steadfastly as I believed other falsehoods. Though yellow attracted me, it made my skin orange. When Dad changed vehicles, he chose red. Maybe I associated all things positive with this vibrant shade. Or does our subconscious know the intrinsic meanings of colors?

My hunger for red grew even stronger when we moved to a house two miles away. Those were days of getting ahead, and Dad worked hard to procure some of the best soil in the state. Our move gave Mom an opportunity to purchase paint, curtains, and carpet. That must have been fun after her hole-in-your-shoe childhood poverty.

At that time, stores promoted a sort of dingy olive with a hint of chartreuse. Women fell for it hook, line, and sinker. In our house, every wall, curtain, carpet, and anything else of fabric made the same drab statement.

My adolescent rebellion involved choosing more and more red. This continued through adulthood, with two short intervals. During my self-denial phase, I "gave up" red for Lent. Methodists made little fuss about Lent, but during my senior year of high school, I discovered *The Nun's Story* in the library where I pored over books and pondered becoming a librarian.

Young girls' sacrifices in the convent drew me. This particular nun went to extremes, and I thought her self-denial noble. If acts of self-abasement could win God's favor, why not?

My propensity for martyrdom loomed. Maybe if I shaved my head, wore long black robes, and knelt on sharp rocks, I could somehow earn forgiveness. This would also be an effortless way to end my problems, since Dad would have killed me if I became a Catholic.

His narrow window of acceptance extended to farmers with English blood, those with barns painted white instead of red. Somehow, he ignored the prolific German blood on Mom's side of the family. Becoming Catholic scared me, not because of the sacrifices, but because of Dad's angry reaction.

Maybe life would get better in college, I thought, so I created my own form of monasticism. In some ways, my rules were more stringent than those I'd read about in the convents. Professors and students alike looked askance at the round-shouldered female doormat who skulked in the back rows of their classes, out of style, out of date, out of hope.

College Bible studies introduced me to the concept of a place for me in the Almighty's broad heart. By my senior year, I returned to wearing red with a passion. I dug out my old rambunctious piano music again. Red signified joy as the realization of my personal worth blossomed.

The other exception to choosing red takes us back to the olive green house where I lobbied for my room to be painted. Upstairs rooms didn't merit coats of paint. Too many rooms, too much expense. So I began my campaign. How could I invite anyone to stay over with an unpainted room?

From the JC Penney's catalog, a picture of a canopied bed, decked with white lace and ruffles, caught my eye. I could live in that bed. Lavender walls surrounded this magnificent piece of furniture, so of course, I wanted lavender for my room. "Lavender? What kind of color was that? Why not a nice green?"

Grandpa, Mom's dad—the one with the hazy mirror—offered to do the work, so the cost amounted to the price of a gallon of paint. Why it took so much pleading and cajoling to accomplish this feat is another story, I suppose, but bottom line, my room probably weighed in at about number six hundred and forty-three on the priority list.

But Grandpa liked me. He even taught me to drive in his 1955 muffler-less red and white Ford. So the paint did finally appear on the walls, but the canopy remained a dream.

Other than that, red reigned for decades, until yellow and grape edged their way in. Yellow signified cheer, because that was the year the buzz saw of the past split open our family. Some of us would survive, while others slunk away into darkness. After that year of horrors, yellow came to stay.

Choosing grape tells another tale. Perhaps coming out of helplessness into empowerment satisfied the need for that bold color. People exclaimed that grape looked wonderful on me with my silvering hair. Grape befits me now. An offshoot of the power color and the royal of purple, the mix reminds me that power and peace coalesce.

Home in a Box

A week before Christmas, I prepare Christmas packages for mailing. Last year at this time, I typed out my thoughts about deployment and facing our first holiday separation in twenty-five years of marriage. Rudyard Kipling's words fit perfectly:

> God gave all men all earth to love,
> but since our hearts are small,
> ordained for each one spot should
> prove beloved over all.

It didn't matter whether the war was popular or not. While my colleagues at the university debated, my husband yearned for a bit of home. While the media questioned our presence in the country, Iraqi citizens sneaked him thank you notes for coming.

"Shukran, Shukran" they wrote. "We will never forget what you have done for us." This heartened him, but still, all he really wanted was a bit of home.

He needed AAA batteries. Many of the troops used AAs, so I sent both. They needed liquid soap, because bars slithered like living creatures out of the makeshift showers into the makeshift sand street where people passed within inches of the shower. Imagine grasping for the elusive soap with your bare, wet arm and hitting a leg.

Rapacious in his longing for lemon-lime Gatorade, dark ground coffee, popcorn, and homemade cookies, he subtly mentioned that he could use more. Within minutes, soldiers decimated piles of pens and notepads, batteries, lip balm, mosquito repellent, and candy set out on a table in his chapel, so he asked for more. The packages weighed so much the sending price far exceeded their value.

I would careen into the post office just before closing, mail a box, and come home to another e-mail saying he ran out of bulbs for his mini-mag reading lamp. Three days and three stores later, I finally procured the specific kind and added the package to another box.

Looking to the largesse of the mail squad for "civilized" needs to be filled, my husband waited. These simple items rendered the 120-degree heat and bumbling bureaucracy manageable.

His tent was dark even in the day, he said, since some of the troops worked at night and slept during daylight hours. Once, reaching into a Christmas tin of his favorite cookies, he felt an extra softness, an additional layer of something fuzzy on the sugary wafers. His flashlight revealed mold.

But these cookies were made by my wife's own hands, he thought. He shut off the light and ate them anyway.

So I kept packaging things we take for granted, but in a place and time where home is parceled out in pieces, insignificant items take on new shape. That summer, I wrote:

> Parceled out in pieces,
> slivers of home
> arrive in remnants.
> I sip small drafts each day,
> boxed, taped, delivered.
> they bring a taste,
> of you—enough
> to remind me
> what is true.

Reminders

During spiritual dry times, seemingly inconsequential reminders bring us back to the reality of God's presence. Emmanuel, God with us, makes for an all-year-long Advent season. Originally, Lance's unit, scheduled to arrive home before Christmas, looked forward to that reunion.

But in September, his unit was informed they wouldn't leave in November as planned. Their deployment extended to a total of 365 days of "boots on the ground," the troops gave the new order a sarcastic label—BOG. Soldiers made painful calls home. Many disappointed children would not see dad or mom at Christmas.

Chaplains work to buoy soldiers' spirits, and this period challenged everyone as morale plummeted. Now they would be in the war zone until February, and the holidays promised an even greater dip in morale. Lance had already set up tables in the makeshift chapel to distribute hundreds of items churches and individuals sent.

Early in the war, a friend of ours from New Mexico spearheaded a church drive to supply soldiers with necessities. As she got the word out, a schoolteacher in the area e-mailed the request to hundreds of schools, resulting in a blizzard of donations.

Another friend from our former parish mailed boxes to Lance and six other soldiers from various units. Her women's group paid the postage and individual members of the congregation contributed. Boxes littered her living room, waiting for the next load of goodies. For the Christmas boxes, she procured a small tree with lights, a filled stocking, and extra treats for each soldier.

An editor who worked with me on several manuscripts

notified churches in Tennessee, and a woman I'd met at a conference years earlier motivated her church headquarters in Georgia to become involved as well.

Most boxes made the December 12 post office deadline, but whether a box arrived before December 25 made little difference. Soldiers worked as usual on holidays, and enjoyed eating homemade cookies well into January.

Only once, a box was not snatched up by the troops. It contained about fifty Christmas cards addressed "to any soldier." A worthy gesture, but apparently none of them perceived themselves as just *any* soldier.

By Name

"I have called you by name," God says in Isaiah 43. That's what I read this morning, and have been pondering the word *name* ever since. Those home-hungry troops longed for word from home, not all-purpose, generic messages.

In the New Testament, the value of the individual explodes before us in living color. God came in a person, one unique individual. Jesus lived and died for the world, yes, but for each of us in particular.

When Jesus chose the twelve to be with Him, He called them by name. Most often, He called himself the Son of Man. This Semitic idiom denotes humanity or self. The Greek *anthropos* translates "Offspring of Man" or "Man's Child."

This is the wonder of the incarnation—He became one of us. He took a human name and lived in our everyday world. He knows what it's like here, and enters into whatever we experience. This truth can see us through dry times, and even through despair.

Self-respect

Mark Twain said it well: "An occasional compliment is necessary to keep up one's self-respect... When you cannot get a compliment any other way, pay yourself one."

But it's tough to pay yourself a compliment when the strongest voice inside you says you're worthless. That voice says you have no right to be here, making adult decisions, because you are inherently flawed, unfit for life, incompetent to go out into the world and seek your fate.

That voice already knows your fate—condemnation, no matter what you do, since the world of shame forbids making a mistake. Human beings make mistakes—in fact, that's how we learn—but you're not allowed to. Your very personhood lies in question.

"How could you have...who do you think you...what right do you have to..." And on and on. It's nauseating, and it never ends.

Does this sound a bit hopeless? Well, actually, I'm writing about hope. To finally accept that this ridiculing, demeaning, humiliating, emasculating voice will never cease attempting to pull us into the nether regions of despair brings hope. We've heard it all before, we'll hear it all again, but—and here's the positive in this—we can stop listening.

I know, it sounds too simple, but I wish I'd appropriated this truth long ago. Just when you think you're doing pretty well, when you've made progress and life looks bright, that slithery, slimy voice straight from the pit raises its ugly head to sneer at you.

"Think you're cool, don't you? You've got people fooled, girl. Well, I see your motivation, and it stinks."

Make one little slip on the path, choose something that goes against your old rigid legalism, and although your head knows better, your heart will condemn you.

For me, self-doubt whispers when I've made the best choice I can. But someone thinks differently. They say it with a smile, for my own good. But their words work within me. Later I look back and realize whoever it was knew my kind. I'm not sure how, but they could detect shame lurking just below the surface of my everyday life, and delighted in wooing it into action.

Such individuals derive joy from destroying the pleasure of shame-based people. The trouble is, we don't realize it at the time. No, as usual, other folks who have dealt with this type of person before have to point out what they so easily see. But we don't "get it" before going through twenty-four hours of shameful hell.

If hell is the absence of God, that period of time comes close. All the Bible verses declaring you a child of God, and that children make mistakes, rattle like prison bars in your mind. Even their power can't get you out of this.

No, shame says you blew it big time, when will you ever learn, there's no possibility of this coming out right, and moreover, you're going to pay. Oh, are you going to pay!

Shame is right about that. The payment is like a toll—you fork out your money for the privilege of traveling the highway. You have to earn the right to drive on to, or get back on, the road.

It doesn't matter that "Jesus paid it all." It doesn't matter that you know He looked at Peter and named him "Rock," or Nathanael and said, "Here's an Israelite in whom there is no guile." That's another world, one in which acceptance and unconditional love come to folks who meet Jesus, and you're not there.

Names meant everything in that world and carried power. The name they gave Christ himself—king of the Jews—ensured his demise on the cross. When I discovered my name means "related by blood" or "Father's joy" the irony struck me—I was related to God. The source of my shame also unknowingly endowed me with a name pointing away from that persistent disturbance.

God calls us beloved, child, even friend. But when shame

unsheathes its sword, everything we know about Him evaporates like water on a blistering hot day. It hangs in the air around us, we know it's true, but we can't appropriate it.

We know we'll survive, that's the good part. We collapse on our beds in the sure understanding that another day will dawn and we'll look back at this and think, *How could I have fallen for that lie again?* We realize, too, that it's been a long time since shame got the better of us.

The periods of joy, peace, and productivity last longer, and the times of utter rejection fade faster. Most of the time, we can give ourselves a compliment. Most of the time, we can look in the mirror and say, "You know what? I like you more every day. You're a beautiful person."

Most days, we can remember that we bring our Father joy, and that hope is our heritage. Most days, we walk with our smile to the sunshine.

Part Seven

Holy Spirit
giving life to all life,
moving all creatures,
root of all things,
washing them clean,
wiping out their mistakes,
healing their wounds,
you are our true life,
luminous, wonderful,
awakening the heart
from its ancient sleep.

~ Hildegard of Bingen
Translated by Stephen Mitchell

Spontaneity

This renovation process drags on and on—things we didn't notice at first form new priorities. As long as we're in the middle of this mess, we might as well do as much as we can. But how can I complain about cleaning and painting a room when last year at this time, I lived alone and mailed care packages to Iraq?

It's fun to imagine how homey this room at the top of the stairs will soon become. Several quirks result from add-ons over the years. On the north end, the ceiling slants down to the wall at a forty-five degree angle for about four feet. A quaint fir-lined cupboard built into the corner connects ceiling to floor. I like its original knobs, bronze coat hooks, and places for shelves along the bottom. We give thanks for small favors: no one painted the inside.

Below the cupboard, two drawers wait to be cleaned, concealing in the empty space below them a bucketful of cement and brick chunks left over from the chimney that used to border the wall. We demolished it to make the bathroom entrance more accessible. Some of this the Shop Vac scooped up, bigger pieces dove down a dark hole next to the heat duct. Hopefully, they came to rest somewhere in the basement walls.

A woman in our town hosts a spring brunch for everyone involved in her semi-annual sales. I went one year, and the women joked that three of them wore rings recycled by another member. The hostess checked their fingers. Yes, those rings all once belonged to her.

Someone next to me gestured toward the kitchen. "Shelly will get tired of those grapevine hangings above her cupboards and put them in the garage sale next spring. I'll probably buy them to replace my enamelware collection I plan on selling at the same sale."

The room filled with good-natured chatter. I sensed the strength around the table. When women get together, there's no end to what can be created, produced, or organized. The power inherent in this group and every similar gathering of women around the world could solve some of our biggest social problems.

If strong women focused on just one conundrum facing our children and grandchildren, the impossible could be accomplished. So many talented, hard-working women like these have crossed my path, and they represent vast potential.

Maybe all our moving during the past few years has brought me to this place, or maybe I'd be in this frame of mind anyway, simply because I'm in my fifties. For whatever reason, the energy in that room impressed me. What can we all contribute in the time left to us on earth?

Julian of Norwich, though she lived a solitary life, still affects people through her writings long after her death. In her nineties, Grace still makes a difference in young women's lives. When women run with an idea, good can come to many, many people.

Positive ideas come into our heads for a purpose. If a brainstorm will enhance someone's life, why did it enter our consciousness? Shouldn't we take action? We can ignore these inspirations, but what might be lost if we do?

In another town where we lived, a woman confided one day, "So many times I've thought of bringing you some homemade pie. But then I think, 'It probably wouldn't be good enough.'"

I stood there wide-eyed, attempting to contain my astonishment.

"Good enough? Do you have any idea what a treat homemade pies are to my family? They don't get homemade dessert very often."

Who knows how a freshly baked pie might have encouraged us on a tough day, and who knows but what the day this lady had the idea was "one of those days" for us. We're talking about mere pies right now, but how tragic to stop listening to the inner guidance we receive!

Maybe we think guidance needs to come cloaked in Bible

verses, with a shivery feeling down our spine. No...divine leading, like a sacrament, often appears in such ordinary forms that we may miss it.

At my first out-of-state convention exhibiting my coping/sympathy card line, I tried too hard to be frugal. The trip propelled me way beyond my comfort zone, but was necessary to launch my grief resources. The expenses of an airline ticket and hotel room haunted me, so I cut down on meals. One meal a day was plenty, I decided. The rest of the time I would cook oatmeal or ramen noodles in my trusty hot pot.

The second day, I staffed my little cardboard display while watching representatives from large companies take turns going out for lunch. Across the aisle sat a pharmaceutical company's lighted display, and during a lull in exhibit traffic, a tall, quiet woman took a seat there. We exchanged smiles. Later, she brought over a delectable-looking chef salad.

"Is there any chance you could eat this?" she asked. "I had the distinct impression I ought to bring lunch for my husband. We live right here in the city, but Frank went out to lunch with some clients. I'm watching the booth for him and have already eaten. Have you?"

That salad sustained me in more ways than one through a long afternoon, and the woman who obeyed her inner impulse spent a great deal of time at my booth. We had much in common. The next day she visited with more food and an invitation. Because my cheap flight required a Saturday night stay, I booked an extra night at the hotel.

"Why don't you check out and stay with us?" she offered. "You can visit our church and we can talk some more."

"Did you ever think," she queried as we walked on Sunday afternoon, "that your card line might be an extension of the mission work you and Lance intended to do years ago? Your cards have the capacity to comfort many people. Maybe your business venture, though uncomfortable right now, fulfills your original calling."

The truth of her words belied the hot afternoon sun on my back. Maybe God's guidance *does* bring shivers. Perhaps in time, the traveling would become routine, the expenditures not so traumatic. Lance's constant sermon, "You have to spend money to make money," might prove true.

This woman's response to one simple thought that came into her mind instructs me even now. What if she had countered the idea to pack a lunch and thought, *Frank can take care of himself. Why should I take a lunch for him?*

What if she had gone about "her own business" that day? I can't speak for her, of course, but for me, a great deal more than a lunch would have been lost.

Compliance

Whoever heard of a building refusing entrance to workers? I can imagine this house saying as we started to knock out walls and create larger spaces:

"Don't you think I'm a little too old for this? A house can get past the point of remodeling, you know? I've sat here for a century and a quarter, who do you think you are to defy the past?"

Unlike humans, houses don't talk back or call a halt to their owners' designs. Isaiah uses a similar metaphor when he mentions the clay questioning its potter (chapter 45). At times, we get disoriented and inquire whether God has forgotten us or lost track of our blueprints.

I doubt Lance and I would have married, had we known each other as teenagers. And I doubt that one of my best friends and I would have realized our "kindred spirits," had we met during my years of traversing those back stairs in our farmhouse. We share important traits, but her independent spirit might not have tolerated my stifling fears.

Gratitude fills me as I recall those lost years, at the mercy of forces I didn't even recognize. To think that the God who created the starry heavens looked down on me then astounds me, still. He sees all of us in our worst periods, yet doesn't turn His back, but coaxes us step by step into an understanding of His love. The brand of coaxing I needed, like a child learning to walk, required a degree of patience foreign to me.

Once we take a few quavering baby steps, we may feel we've come a long, long way. But the divine work continues—we need vast renovation. What a mystery that the Creator of the universe would focus on us in the same way Lance and I now attend to this old house, and what a miracle.

Today I meditated on John 3:17, and the KJV I memorized as a baby Christian flooded my mind. "For God sent not his Son to condemn the world, but that the world through Him might be saved." The word *not* stood out to me. Did not send. God's purpose was not to condemn.

Some of us grow up with the equivalent of a Ph.D. in punishment, but so did John Bunyan. John and I have a lot in common. His *Grace Abounding to the Chief of Sinners* gave me hope when I thought my waywardness might be too much for God to handle.

The first time I read the Gospel of John, I stopped on the "not." For so long, I had trembled that God would cast me out, but this verse explained just the opposite. God didn't send His Son to condemn us. I could hardly take it in. Jesus didn't come to punish?

Then where did my fear originate? Why did I quake so at the thought of my Creator? Why was it so difficult to believe He loved and wanted me just as I was? I was eighteen. I hadn't had time to look back, or I would have known the answers. I had no idea of the shadow's depth in which I stood. What I called my *lack of faith* produced even more guilt.

Sometimes, it's good to look back. Not to stay there, but to scan that bleak, hopeless horizon, knowing that our God saw us, knew our pain, and already set plans in motion to meet our needs. On the radio yesterday, a preacher lauded the incredible forgiveness Christ offers us, the lengths to which God went to reveal his forever love.

I listened until the end of the sermon, where the speaker threw in a couple of sentences that seemed out of place and unnecessary. "But terrible punishment waits if we don't..."

Does it? Isn't separation from love and light enough punishment for any frail human being? Does God wait with His razor strap (as my grandfather waited for my dad) or His leather belt and buckle (as Dad waited for me) if we don't or can't respond? Is He, after all, like a raging human father?

Julian of Norwich visualizes a God without harshness. Hildegard of Bingen describes the Holy Spirit's work of waking us up and bringing us out of darkness, "...moving all creatures... washing them clean, wiping out their mistakes, healing their wounds..."

Can you visualize a great loving hand sweeping toward our woeful world, tenderly swabbing away our shortcomings? That hand spreads warmth and light and compassion. For God sent *not* His only Son to condemn the world... Yes. Yes. Come, Holy Spirit.

The Attic

Attics always interest me, especially the kind you see in movies, stacked with boxes and trunks full of treasures from bygone days. This house has no such spacious attic, only crawl spaces that lure bats. The night disperses their noises, and no amount of insulation deters them. So far, that is.

On the farm, we had a spectacular attic complete with an antique Edison Victrola, metal ice skates that attached to the bottoms of boots, an ancient iron bedstead, carved antique picture frames, and a set of old oak chairs. Unlike the attics in the cinema, there was no order to the airy, dusty space. Everything lay hither and yon; you might find an old copper ladle in a heap of discarded wood.

Best of all, the attic provided a great view of the country for miles around. The south view gave me a perfect lookout as thunderstorms propelled themselves across fields as flat and fragile as window glass. Once, a tornado pummeled the fence west of our pine grove, but I wasn't home at the time.

In my late teens, I spent too much time up there, tracking tremendous summer storms with their gallant flashes of lightning and barreled thunder. I found nature's convolutions invigorating, but life itself frightened me beyond action. Terrified of going to college, I thought maybe I could stay up there and write like Emily Dickinson.

The word *recluse* intrigued me. I could live shut up in this apartment-sized attic and write and write and whatever else my young heart desired. Even with its piles of dead bees and my severe dust allergy, something about the space summoned me.

Candy Wilson and I spent hours here in junior high, pawing through corners and piles of boards scattered with antiques. This hideaway attracted her, too. Her family lived in a large, clean, square house in town, not as exciting as our run-down seventeen-room ex-mansion. Something akin to a pioneer spirit hovered in our surreptitious explorations. No one else understood the old grungy garret's fascination, but Candy did.

Also smitten with Mom's homemade noodles, this friend exclaimed over the egg and flour creations that left you with a satisfied sense of strength for whatever lay ahead. Even now, I mix, roll out, cut, and plop the fat strips into boiling chicken broth when someone has a bad sore throat or cold, or when I need some comfort food.

To think that Candy would like not just one, but two things about my home! Her natural good looks and pleasing personality attracted many friends. I couldn't believe it when she agreed to stay overnight with me. The most popular girl in our class, she could have politely refused. That would have devastated me, since I had to beg to have her over. Mom didn't like the idea of people staying all night.

But Candy came, and then she invited me to her house, where we curled on her bed to pore over old knitting magazines. We giggled at the absurd fashions women used to wear. Maybe that's what drew us to the attic.

A 1913 Sears and Roebuck fashion catalog with the latest styles out of Chicago sprawled on the floorboards up there. We propped the weighty book on two chairs to peruse the pages. It was about two feet high and eighteen inches wide, with a heavy dark green hardback cover.

We leafed through scenes of days gone by, replete with gay young blades, lovely ladies on their arms. Pinstriped suits and bright wide ties, outlandishly beribboned dresses, everything down to these people's shoes, brought peals of laughter. It doesn't get better than two friends chortling together.

Candy really shouldn't have taken a second look at me, but if she hadn't, my social life would have dwindled by ninety-five percent. Because of her, the other "in" girls accepted me. They discovered I could write poetry on the spot, so I became the group's unlikely court jester.

Years later at a class reunion when we talked about the old

days, Candy mentioned the attic, along with the noodles. Mom's health had begun to fail, and it was good to tell her that her cooking made an impression on Candy, the lawyer's daughter, the slight, athletic girl with long, thick pigtails and freckles who became a beautiful teenager, the high school homecoming queen, a person with a future.

Those lighthearted times play a role in my memories, but more often, later recollections emerge. At some point, acceptance in our high school group couldn't possibly assuage my growing self-hatred. I hungered for a deeper sort of acceptance, but at the same time, doubted such unconditional love existed.

What could possibly be my purpose in life, anyway? How could I function in this world? When a guy asked me to dance, self-consciousness and fear prevented me from saying yes. What did I have to offer anyone?

At the entrance to adulthood, I was seventeen, finished with high school. A college had accepted me, and there was so much ahead to learn. Anticipation rather than dread should fill me now. Instead, I spent more and more time at the top of the house, where the smell of rain enticed me to scan for thunderstorms and consider Emily Dickinson.

Mercy

Recently I read an encouragement from a saint of old that bought back the attic years. At that time, swamped by near-despair, little did I know what good things God had in store. Little did I understand Shakespeare's "unstrained quality of mercy, dropping as the gentle rain from heaven."

> So let us not trouble ourselves about our
> fears.
> Nor lose heart at the sight of our frailty,
> But humbly remind ourselves that without
> the grace of God
> we are nothing.
> And then, distrusting our own strength,
> Let us commit ourselves to His mercy.
> Follow Jesus into the Garden of Gethsemane
> and on to Calvary.
> And only then to Easter morning.
> ~ Saint Teresa of Avila

What did I know of Easter morning? What did I know of distrusting my own strength? Oh, I would have agreed that I was nothing, but not in the way Saint Teresa intended. Seeing no value whatsoever in oneself does God no favors.

Did I distrust my own strength? Even when we choose despair, we trust in our own strength. We will not allow another to lift us up because we trust our valuation of circumstances rather than God's. He declares us worthy of His own Son's death, but we beg to disagree.

And commitment? What did I know of committing myself?

I would find out. The good news would come to me through a book, which tells me that God goes to whatever lengths He must to reach us. Unlike people who might have shared the Gospel with me, a book was unintimidating. Words on a page, I could handle.

That summer after graduation, I consumed Catherine Marshall's *Beyond Ourselves*. In chapter six, the author described the gift of knowing God's love and forgiveness as there for the taking. I knelt on the floor beside the bed and pleaded with God, a first tentative step out of the realm of shame into the light.

Catherine said to read the Bible, so I did, and still remember the text making sense for the first time, as if written with my particular questions in mind. I wanted to move faster into faith, but had no idea what held me down. I labeled it sin, but over time have come to see it more shame. For me, being unworthy of such love translated into total worthlessness, abject depravity with no inkling of good.

The deep meaning of Saint Teresa's words unfolded only difficult years later. I *did* trouble myself about my fears, I *did* lose heart at the sight of my frailty. I despaired of ever coming into God's kingdom, and every time I doubted, I flagellated myself some more. Why couldn't I believe? Why couldn't I commit my destiny to this kind Father?

James Joyce describes errors as portals of discovery. But what could floundering in a sea of doubt and trepidation open up for me? What could break this cycle of sin and shame, like a merry-go-round with no joy? I was so afraid of making an error, I couldn't move.

People commit themselves to causes, to mental wards, to marriage partners. To the best of my ability—and there's a comment on our own strength—I did commit myself to God. Yet I didn't begin to comprehend His commitment to me.

That challenge still remains. When One incapable of lying or deceiving makes a commitment, the discussion moves to another realm, since our concept of dedication falls so far short of God's binding pledge. As another of our layers of shame strips away, we lift our heads and find Him still true to His promise. Never-ending love spellbinds our hearts. And then we go on to yet another layer.

Saint Teresa's life story, wild and complicated, burgeons with adversaries and troubles of all sorts. No wonder she became the patron saint of those who suffer headaches. She knew firsthand what it meant to commit herself to God's mercy after her father's strict rules, her mother's death when she was young, and a severe case of malaria that almost killed her.

When she had her first visions during prayer, the clergy discouraged her by proclaiming them of the devil. Finally, when she was forty-one, a priest encouraged her to implore God to return, and the Spanish Inquisition scrutinized her for deviation from orthodox religious experience.

When she complained to God, she heard Him say, "That is how I treat all my friends." At forty-three, Teresa sought to establish a new order, but again met with disapproval from the powers-that-be. She prevailed, however, and her order commits to poverty and simplicity, but even then, a papal representative called her "a restless disobedient gadabout."

"The important thing is not to think much but to love much and so do that which best stirs you to love..." If ever a saint's comments applied to me, it would be this, since it reflects the teaching of Proverbs 3:5-6, "Lean not unto thine own understanding" (KJV). I memorized that verse during college, but applying it will take a lifetime.

That which best stirs you to love. Oh, my. I sit at my computer today, totally engaged in this vocation of writing. I knew during middle school that writing was my best outlet, but I lacked the self-confidence to pursue God's gift. "Still, there is time," He whispers.

"As for me, the nearness of God is my good" (Psalm 73:28, NASB). Someone gave me this verse once, in concern for my consistent wandering to condemnation and punishment. At the time, I desired God's nearness, but my fears hindered trust in His mercy. In the practice of Lectio Divina, I stay with this word—*mercy*. For the rest of my life, let me rest in mercy.

Merciful Eyes

"It is not what you are nor what you have been
that God sees with His all-merciful eyes,
but what you desire to be."

The Cloud of Unknowing, translated by William Johnston

All-merciful eyes change everything. Cherubim, eyes everywhere, cry, "Holy, Holy, Holy." But these words speak of merciful eyes. Mercy, Mercy, Mercy.

I have known merciful eyes—yes, dark brown ones, hiding me behind a skirt—shielding, protecting, standing between me and the piercing blue of condemning eyes.

More than anything, we longed for acceptance. More than anything, most of us dread rejection. "Blessed are those who hunger and thirst." Oh, I did! And Jesus heard my heart's cry. He heard, and through my mother, He comforted my childhood tears. Later, He kept me in life through those devastating years when I believed God would act toward me like my father.

But even now, I don't always claim the reality of unconditional love instead of my own perceptions. Old Testament wrath and recrimination juxtapose with tender care for Israel, yet I see undiluted elements. Love and hate, mercy and wrath, kindness and severity...I see in a mirror dimly.

Oh, to believe You watch with all-merciful eyes... compassionate, kind, understanding eyes, for You know our frame, and remember we are dust. Our feebleness, our foibles, our shortcomings do not surprise You. My perversity of perception...You know it through and through.

In Christ, we are made holy and blameless, Ephesians

tells us so. Why such effort to believe we're in no danger of Your vengeance? You are well aware that the expectations of our youth die hard deaths. You see us through shed blood, blameless, clean. Will we ever fully grasp Your mercy?

Teach our wounded hearts about Your all-merciful eyes. Infuse in us a new concept of those eyes, waiting for us without recrimination, without blame, without impatience, without anger, without harshness, without rage.

All-merciful eyes...completely, thoroughly merciful. Omniscient, ever-merciful eyes, windows to Your love. Unchanging eyes, compassionate, kind, meeting us in the baggage created by a dearth of mercy. The prophet Isaiah says You wait to show us mercy (chapter 30).

Help us believe someone waits, and watches...someone kind, good-intentioned, good-natured, forgiving, sustaining. Change our image of You. Help us receive.

Let us stay here on our landing to meet You anew. Unselfish, ready to meet needs, never stingy or withholding gifts from Your beloved children. Re-route our senses, re-distribute the neurons, refresh our spirits, revitalize our perspective, O merciful-eyed One. Let us see You with new eyes.

Kaleidoscope

"O thou afflicted, tossed with tempest, [and] not comforted, behold, I will lay thy stones with fair colours, and lay thy foundations with sapphires" (Isaiah 54:11, KJV).

Fair colors, sapphire foundations...this part of Isaiah abounds in poetry and beauty. I didn't realize until a few years ago that one of God's main attributes is beauty. Love, mercy, justice, sovereignty, omniscience...I would have listed those if asked, but beauty? Somewhere along the way, I missed that teaching.

When I called our bank this morning, their hold service gave waiting customers interesting facts about nature. Flamingos, the voice assured listeners, are not born pink. My search revealed that baby flamingos are indeed a plain white. Their color develops as they eat blue and green algae.

Why do they turn pink? A chemist could explain, but for our purposes, it's enough to know the result. Not only do flamingos' feathers transform as they eat small crustaceans containing beta-carotene, but the depth of their coloring depends on where they live. Chilean species exhibit only a faint pink tinge, while Caribbean flamingos turn vermillion or crimson.

What does this have to do with growth, God's word for me today? Just before I connected with the voice on the phone, I read Jesus's parable of the sower whose seed landed in various types of soil.

Life was inherent in the seeds, but where they fell made all the difference. Mix rich soil and seed, and you harvest a great crop. But scatter seed to the wind and you reap the wind. Toss seed onto poor soil—rocky, dry, or weedy—to your sorrow. Seed has to take root, and plants need room to grow.

The same is true with people. A certain mix is necessary

for our spirits to flourish. If we fail to receive the necessary nurturing, stunted growth results, although time and love can redeem our loss. Even if we have a history of giving our power to others, thereby evading responsibility for ourselves, we can change.

One woman finally realized her skewed thinking when her friend said, "When you say only your dad's and your husband's opinions of you matter, you call the rest of us liars. We look at you and see competence, attractiveness, and value, but you seem determined to listen only to the negative voices. You've made two individuals into gods and the rest of us into chopped liver."

Ouch!

"Faithful are the wounds of a friend" (Proverbs 27:6, KJV).

Recently, I discovered that jasper is the gem of nurturing. An Arizona hike introduced me to the stone. Before that time, I referenced this precious stone only from the book of Revelation, where jasper forms the first foundation of the new city of Jerusalem (chapter 21). Jasper also joined eleven other stones to create Aaron's priestly breastplate designed through God's mountaintop instructions to Moses.

Why did it matter to God that those particular gems adorn the priest? Wouldn't any old kind of rock have worked just as well? Why such meticulous attention to detail regarding the service of the temple, with stonecutters, carvers, and artisans devoting such time and energy to the outcome? Why turn flamingos into such flamboyant colors?

Andreas, bishop of Caesurae in the tenth century, linked each of the twelve stones given to Moses with one of the Apostles. The stones correspond to various personal qualities, jasper in particular to power and personal responsibility. For example, jasper is believed to encourage one to speak out from a sense of grounding and healthy independence.

I explored further, to find which Apostle the Bishop paired with which precious stone. Intuition told me he matched jasper with Saint Peter, and voilà! Who could so closely incorporate all the qualities associated with jasper—transformation, empowerment, and nurture—but Peter? It took intense growth for him to move from impetuous fisherman to caring shepherd.

Even some twelve-step programs reference precious stones to the steps, and it's not too surprising to learn that jasper parallels Step Eight, in which participants make a list of everyone they have harmed and become willing to make amends. Progressing to this point takes time and focus and empowers the participant.

In ancient times, warriors and kings used jasper, too, with an obvious connection to power and protection. Loyalty marks warriors, who stand up for their principles and go to battle for what they believe is right. Is it any wonder that jasper was thought to help persons facing necessary change, and specifically victims?

A breastplate supplies protection. When we face pivotal decisions, we need protection not only from others, but also from ourselves. Our greatest enemy, as Winston Churchill memorialized during the Second World War, is fear itself. In victim mode, we sometimes tremble before an enemy, only to discover our fear was exaggerated.

The variety of jasper stones we saw on our hike south of Payson shone red and orange in the sun. Jasper can also be yellow, tan, brown, green gray, blue, and black. A rock hound on the hike showed us another quality that sets this gem apart. In a world of ragged, rough rocks, jasper is smooth, like rocks tumbled in a polisher.

I bet this will lead us to suffering. And yes, research reveals that jasper is tough cryptocrystalline quartz, its mineral crystals invisible except with a powerful microscope. Common in many areas of the world, quartz covers about twelve percent of the earth, and jasper contains impurities from other rocks that give it various colors.

Mighty forces of wind and climate break rocks and integrate all these tiny bits of mineral into quartz, producing jasper. It's a drastic, traumatic transformation, resulting in hard-won beauty. If rocks had feelings, I think Jasper would shed tears, but like people struggling their way to empowerment, its surface sports a sheen.

I brought a few samples home to wash and display. Some jasper gems embedded in larger rocks, and some bore crosses or crisscrosses of bold, white filling. We hikers all agreed on one thing—jasper is beautiful. That spells hope for us in a spiritual sense. Beauty dances through creation, from various shades of flamingos to variegated rocks.

Isaiah 54:11 comforted and intrigued me when I first read the book. God's plan for our lives incorporates beauty? It was too much to take in at the time. But our Creator lavishes color and uniqueness on creation, and that includes humankind. We find this long-range plan difficult to remember during our "tumbling" phases, but the beauty and meaning surrounding us in nature provide a reminder.

God? Aggressive?

What list of divine qualities contains aggression, along with righteousness, omnipotence, faithfulness, glory, holiness, and grace? Aggression, one of those negatively charged words, doesn't fit our God, does it? Assertive, perhaps, but aggressive?

Yet one synonym of aggression, forcefulness, links closely with power. And Heaven knows, a clear picture of God's proactivity on our behalf would amend many of our woes. What if we believed Francis Thompson's description of this God—The Hound of Heaven?

Theology causes a problem, especially for Protestants, since we're accustomed to the Divine Seeker standing at our heart's door awaiting our invitation. In college, someone told me God would not barge in on us, an attitude revealing the opposite of aggression. But this Father takes action to draw human beings into awareness of His presence.

My word today: Exodus 6:7. "I will take you as my people, and I will be your God." *To take* portrays choice, premeditated action, and a fine line between force and passion.

The Message uses "aggressive forgiveness" as a synonym for grace in Romans 5:20-21:

> All that passing laws against sin did was produce more lawbreakers. But sin didn't, and doesn't, have a chance in competition with the aggressive forgiveness we call grace. When it's sin versus grace, grace wins hands down. All sin can do is threaten us with death, and that's the end of it. Grace, because God is putting everything together again through the Messiah, invites us into life—a life that goes on and on and on, world without end.

So, grace equals aggressive forgiveness? That has a ring to it, and the phrase takes me back forty years, to a chaotic household of hardworking farm people. For one member of the family, *grace* was an idea from church, foreign and tantalizing.

But the concept tiptoes into her consciousness. Could the eternal God possibly want her? Could such hope, the tantalizing possibility of life without fear, be real? Can an adolescent so convinced of her worthlessness discover, like Cinderella, that someone values her beyond her wildest imagination?

Voracious, she reads more. She prays again and again, without realizing this Father responded to her soul's cry long ago. He has "taken" her as one of His people, and promised to be her God. Such a truth is too much right now, but she hopes her voice carries to heaven.

Years pass, and she studies Scripture's astonishing promises. She meditates, memorizes, absorbs, doubts, meditates, memorizes, absorbs some more, and doubts some more.

Through human kindness, her grip on what she sees as God's requirements loosens. In spite of her commitment to this God who has taken her, many of her days and nights fill with striving after acceptance and serenity. Scripture proclaims her God's beloved child, but she longs for more faith.

She works hard to stop working for what cannot be earned. It's a tough habit to break—earning is the only way she knows. More years pass, allowing her to learn release, to quiet her tumultuous heart under protection that does not fail, to realize both the truth and the deception that binds her.

Her determination to grow, to please, to perform, to become who she ought to be yields some fruit, but little by little, the light overtakes her striving, and her constant vigilance yields. She learns to listen and respond rather than feel eternally responsible. She relies less on antiquated defenses. She accepts, bit by bit, her freedom as God's own. Little by little, liberty nests in her spirit.

She discovers her gifts, and the world's need for what she can offer. Her growing confidence highlights her capabilities, the joyful potential of her personhood, in ways contrary to those unspoken rules she once followed. She belongs because God took her, not because of anything she did. God took her because He created her, because of love. She belongs, in spite of falterings, failings, and fears.

This God asks only for receptivity, and she wants to be receptive. She learns to *be*, nothing more, as she responds and rests. Any inkling of control she cherished was illusion. She discovers that the most deceptive of enemies—fear itself—fears change the most, even change for the better.

Who would not long for freedom from an inner voice that declares her inadequate, hopeless, unworthy, unlovable? Who would not lean into a compassion that knows her powerlessness, her tendency for blame, her weary, effort-laden spirit? It will be an arduous journey to complete liberty from fear's tenacious effects, a long leap to letting go, but the taste of love sits well. She will keep traveling.

Ineffable, exotic, gently forceful love created her, sought her, wooed her, and ignited her beginning speck of faith. Is *gently forceful* an oxymoron? No, this love reached out with tender care and came to dwell within one riddled by fear. The initiative divine, the timing and planning assertive, God's "taking" produced release beyond comprehension.

Then, in spite of her, this divine affection that took her proceeded to work in and through her for the sheer joy of it. Aggressive forgiveness—without it, where would she be?

Poetry

Throughout adolescence and my college years, I fell into poetry binges, a frustrated, would-be writer. Always, verses surfaced when I took pencil and paper in hand. Why would rhymes, meters, and the flow of words so entrance a farmer's daughter perched on the edge of unthinkable dreams? No one in our family, with the possible exception of Uncle Ed in his singing, dealt in words' nuances and subtleties.

Mom died on December 31.The funeral sermon mentioned the original meaning and spelling of *Noel*—Nowell. Now all is well. Mom suffered in many ways during her last few years. Now she could rest, pain-free.

On our hurried trip, I sensed her presence. Before she breathed her last, Mom saw her mother. "It was no hallucination," the hospital chaplain said. "She *sees* her mother now." That picture, relayed by telephone, comforted me, and as we drove halfway across the nation, Mom traveled with us:

> Moving from the mountains
> to the plains, you were there, but
> not as you left this world.
> No. Young, vibrant-eyed, in your
> graduation photograph—that's
> how you will remain.
> Heartaches spent,
> unspoken dreams and
> swallowed fears whisked into
> brightness, past the scope
> of wondering.
> Into the arms of God's vast
> timeless sea, the only place

final peace can be.

Now all was well. Not for me, though. During my morning walk in the basement of an older university building on the coldest days that winter, like a steady beat, poetry, my old friend, trailed along with me, words with footsteps.

In the stillness before anyone arrived for work, I thumped through the echoing halls, up and down wide old stairways with worn wooden rails, words pulsing.

Early Morning

Down in a building's bowels
a woman walks under pipes that
consistently weep, down where
the furnace's hiss and the sounds
of intake whisper wisdom
in a place bleak and
stark to the untrained eye.
She listens, arms held
aerobically high. In the
silence before dawn, she's walking,

and sometimes in hope,
sometimes in sorrow,
she's talking.

What was she saying? My heart, a maze of guilt and grace, longed for more consolation than a funeral sermon could give. Why couldn't I have tried harder, been better, loved more?

The comfort initiated during those hours on the road returned to sift into my soul. Biding its time, comfort, like true love, won't be forced. Waiting just outside the courtyard, comfort sidles inward until one day, you find traces in your senses, footprints on the walls of your pain.

Part Eight

"Artistic temperament sometimes seems a battleground, a dark angel of destruction and a bright angel of creativity wrestling."

~ Madeleine L'Engle

Who We Are

Searching in vain for the right picture to hang above our couch, I began to think some sort of fabric hanging might work. One night as I dug around in the lower part of the buffet for tablecloths and napkins, my hand touched a placemat. I remembered buying it, store sticker still in place, at a garage sale last fall. In the print of a primitive painting, a large, red brick house sided by two round-topped trees sat above a verse from Proverbs: "By wisdom a house is built, and by understanding it is established; by knowledge the rooms are filled with rare and beautiful treasures."

I fished out an antique frame from basement storage to see if the two would work together. They did, and a few hours later, I waited in a gallery dedicated to the works of a local artist while her nephew matted my rummaged treasure. With ample time to read about the artist's life in volumes composed by surviving relatives, I gave thanks this woman's story did not die with her.

Born just after the turn of the century, she knew her artistic calling when she created her first flower at age eight. She never lost that vision, although loved ones stood in the way of her dream.

Her mother could not understand her desire to study art when a teaching career made such sense, so she earned a teaching degree and taught in rural schools. Because of her father's openness, she eventually studied art so that she was able to teach what she loved for twenty years in Detroit. She never stopped painting. At least two young men courted her, but she chose her art.

After retirement, she moved to New York, where she lived until age ninety-one. For forty years, she filled her small apartment with paintings, which she stacked from floor to ceiling, all the while showing her work to galleries as she sought one to book a one-woman show. None showed interest, but rejection did not deter her.

She took many of her meals at a small neighborhood delicatessen where she found "family." When she turned ninety, this family who by now claimed her dream, became instrumental in its fulfillment. A display of her work filled the little eating establishment, and one day a representative for a promotional company stopped. Struck by her paintings, he signed on to the dream.

With his help, in 1988, this woman's lifelong outpouring displayed solo at the National Arts Club in Gramercy Park. Many paintings sold during that showing, and today her work can be viewed and purchased at galleries both in New York City and her hometown.

Some penciled notes in the artist's own hand fill four pages of one of the gallery's albums. "Our minds are our essence," she writes, "and God promises to make everything new." She determines to create each day.

Immersed in the beauty this strong woman gave the world, I breathed a little more deeply the air of my own aspirations. The thoughts that come to us, the intentions we organize, the goals we set, those beginnings of dreams about who we'll become, outline our future. As children, we played with them as toys, but perhaps we lacked courage to pursue them when the time came.

Maybe we squelched them at someone else's insistence. At some point, those dreams may haunt us, and we regret piddling around with them. Anything short of embracing dreams does no justice to our gifts, brings no glory to our Creator.

What of a woman spending her life—her whole, long life—creating paintings? What if her canvasses remained undiscovered, never appreciated by an enthusiastic clientele? Was her joy in becoming "known" equal to her joy in creating, throughout all those long years she spent alone in her apartment?

Does working in obscurity obliterate the beauty of the work?

I used to think people were meant to seek "God's will," as if this entity existed outside us, and wafted in from an unknown place. Now I see that guidance comes through our minds and spirits, as God's Word counsels us.

In Matthew five, Jesus teaches:

> "You're blessed when you're at the end of your rope. With less of you there is more of God and His rule. You're blessed when you feel you've lost what is most dear to you. Only then can you be embraced by the One most dear to you. You're blessed when you're content with just who you are—no more no less. That's the moment you find yourselves proud owners of everything that can't be bought" (MSG).

Perhaps our shortcomings weigh too heavily to start over. We may recognize that our determined efforts have worsened our problems instead of helped. Maybe we have hurt others and ourselves beyond reconciliation, and finally acknowledge that we can blame no one else. A dead end looms.

I think our artist friend would hold those pieces in her hands and say, "I'm not dead yet." Al-Anon's sixth step says we are now entirely ready to have our character defects removed. We are in position for God to act, to let go of our efforts and watch divine creativity work. We are finally at the beginning.

The design of our ideal epitaph lies within us, sometimes smashed down by well-meaning but destructive loved ones' good intentions, sometimes curtailed by our awkward reticence to claim our gifts, sometimes silenced by our terror and shame. But inklings whispering why we were born never leave us. Our life's work weaves through God's continued creation of us as unique individuals.

Create in Me...

A man faced the error of his ways locked inside his bank's vault late on a Christmas Eve afternoon. His captivity lasted thirty-six hours. He survived because a small hole allowed air to enter, and when a worker unlocked his prison the day after Christmas, he slipped out unobserved.

He gulped water and went home to wash and change clothes. When he came back to work, he realized no one missed him. Wanting an "unbothered" Christmas, he turned down an invitation for Christmas Eve, and another for Christmas Day. His forced encounter with himself, like Scrooge's, shifted his life like an earthquake.

"Create in me a clean heart, O God, and renew a right spirit within me." The very first word arrests us. If we really mean it when we pray "Create in me," a whole new world opens. The thing is, we have no clue what God will work in us, once that creative power is unleashed.

Look what our Creator has made: a vast universe beyond human comprehension, an earth teeming with infinitesimal variety, human bodies so complicated researchers stand in awe. We are already "fearfully and wonderfully made" (Psalm 139, KJV). How might the Almighty transform us if we ask for a clean heart, a new and right spirit?

Al-Anon's sixth step, "become ready" for God to remove our character defects, cozies up to today's word *create*. When we come to this place, we've had it with our own analyses and bumbling attempts to control or fix others and ourselves. Our efforts have gotten us nowhere, or somewhere very painful. We recognize them as pride-filled lunacy.

Einstein's definition of insanity trots across our consciousness--doing the same thing over and over, yet expecting different results. There we go. There we are. Like the banker, we feel trapped by what we've done to ourselves while a sublime force holds us at attention.

We wait before the God in whom we say we believe. But it's still scary to mouth the word *create* because we don't know what our cry will produce. It's an ending. It means we're finished, kaput. It means we let go of our grip and humble ourselves. Those three words echo through our souls, a web that catches us. "Create in me..."

It's also a beginning. Like a house under renovation or a patient entering surgery, we hear the lights flick on, the tools readied. We tremble, yet trust. We've moved to the seventh step. We've asked God to create, and we have become watchers.

What a change in perspective—the banker came out of the safe a new person. Chances are, he engaged with his co-workers and acquaintances during the next year. When December rolled around, maybe he even invited everyone to his place. Those were *his* changes, a transformation utterly beyond his imagination.

How will we change? That's the thing. We don't know. We're on an adventure, and we simply let God work.

Afterword

Postludes provide an emotional pocket much like a landing, a spot to pause. After the holiday season, we meditate on Herod's slaughter of Bethlehem's male children two and under. This vicious crime brings us up short. After all the excitement of Christmas, we don't want to think about murdered children.

Herod the Great accomplished some outstanding feats, such as rebuilding the temple in Jerusalem. Another of his structures, the Wailing Wall, still stands today. Although quite the builder, Herod's family life left something to be desired. He killed his wife, his three sons, his mother-in-law, brother-in-law, uncle, and many others.

He also committed some atrocities in his public life, motivated by insecurity and egocentricity. One of them was killing all the little boys around Bethlehem when he discovered the prophesied Messiah's birthplace.

Why, why, why, I wonder, did the wise men have to go through Jerusalem? These Persians played a part in the fulfillment of the many prophecies surrounding Jesus's birth as they came to worship the Messiah. But why did they have to ask for directions in Jerusalem, so that King Herod heard about this potential threat to his throne?

Matthew tells us that "all of Jerusalem"—probably meaning everyone in power with Herod—felt terror when the Eastern scholars arrived.

Had they wandered about the countryside a while longer in their search, maybe they could have found some other kind of guidance. After all, they followed a star this far to the general vicinity. Why couldn't they continue to follow that light to Bethlehem? Does my longing come through to wipe out this story from the Gospels? Intrigue and murder and the comfortless wailing of mothers ought to have no place in the amazing story of the baby Jesus sleeping on sweet hay.

We ask the same kind of questions in the aftermath of contemporary horrors. Of course, no answers exist, but the curious spirit within us must ask, anyway. We fall into this kind of thinking often. "These people are Christians. Why should this terrible accident befall their child?" Or "How could someone in our family do such a hurtful thing?"

Reading Matthew's account, we ask, "Couldn't this wonderful, earth-shattering event have occurred without babies being murdered? What about these other parents who wept inconsolably for their tiny boys, even as God so carefully, in the midst of all this danger, protected Mary, Joseph, and their precious infant?"

But the facts are, the arrival of God's Son is fraught with human power hunger, deceit, and conspiracy.

After the wise men consulted Herod in Jerusalem, Matthew says the star reappeared (chapter 2). After they followed the celestial guidance to Jerusalem, did the star disappear? Why? Did God switch off its light for a time? Why didn't ruthless Herod follow the men from the East straight to Jesus and kill Him on the spot?

Perhaps we should ask, instead, how Jesus escaped evil so intent on destroying Him. The shepherds saw the star at His birth. The wise men followed it for months from far away. Did other people see it too? Or was faith a prerequisite for sight? Perhaps angels prevented Herod and his soldiers from viewing the star.

Our speculations come to rest on one of the meanings of the child's name: Emmanuel, God with us, right in the midst of such terror and bloody agony. For the intellectually honest, this juxtaposition of life and death, hope and sorrow ushers in belief. No fairy-tale dust sparkles in the air when babies lie dead, their mothers keening in unspeakable sorrow. Those who consider this story with integrity must include the slaughter of the innocent.

The virgin birth troubles some people, but a real king named Herod, about whom we know much from recorded history, did indeed murder Bethlehem's little ones. What would motivate him, if not paranoiac fear of losing what mattered most to him? A realist, this monarch believed another king lay out there in Judah.

So we have miracle and murder, power and weakness, protection and pain. Despite all our political, sociological, and technological advances, the scenario sounds all too familiar.

We balance these ambivalent concepts in our fragile minds. In humility, understanding only partially, we consider the aftermath of Christmas, the prelude to Easter.

Embracing

In this waiting-for-spring season, my rumination centers on one thought: "Instead of redoubling our efforts, we simply embrace what the Holy Spirit is doing in us" (Romans 7 MSG). From this verse, the word *embrace* becomes the focus.

Synonyms for embrace include hug, draw close, and encircle tightly. Images of a leave taking or a homecoming, or perhaps a forgiving, come to mind. Embracing can involve a time lapse as we step back to look into each other's eyes, then re-enfold another, as did the prodigal's father.

The enfolding need not be mutual. A baby or young child lets itself be taken in by larger arms (and we're to become as children). Another element of an embrace: we do not want to let go, or have the other person let go of us.

Our thesaurus adds cling, hold in your arms, cuddle, squeeze, clinch. There is no such animal as an embrace apart from attitudes of acceptance and inclusion. The term *empty embrace* contradicts itself.

To embrace is to zero in on, to focus all of one's attention. We can't embrace someone while attending to another activity at the same time. Holding someone close consumes all thought and energy. Enveloping a friend or loved one supplants other actions. In fact, a stronger synonym for *embrace* is to devour.

During our granddaughter's infancy, this concept crystallized. Nearly asleep in my arms, her presence erased all other thoughts as we lullabyed to sleep. Her eyelids fluttered, azure eyes opened and closed, then opened...then closed. Finally, her breathing deepened in total trust. She held my rapt attention. Immersed in each other, we rested there, content in quiet closeness.

No difficulty exists in such a state. It's simple. Simply embracing. Holding close what the Holy Spirit is doing in our lives pulls us out of self-effort into serenity, out of determination into receptivity, out of time into eternity. In this letting go, I admit my lack of knowledge and discard all illusion of control.

In my mental rocker, the word of God, the Spirit's work in my being, enfolds me. Simply. Basically, purely, mainly, only. Perhaps I hold close only one word: beloved. Letting go is not my strong suit, but my breathing deepens.

The metaphor blossoms as I exchange places with my beautiful grandchild and release my concerns about the future, even those about the person I'm becoming. Simply embracing throws all anxiety onto the Father, completely present and competent.

I become my granddaughter, held in loving arms. Like a child, I trust the embracer without analyzing, planning, administrating, suggesting, withholding, working, striving, worrying, stressing, or struggling, I release myself into God's focused travail on my behalf. Simply embracing.

Wooden Spoons and Prayer

It's a new month, one month closer to spring's warmth and light. Our house cooperates most of the time now, so we keep checking off goals. I visit that little room at the top of the stairs every once in a while, especially when afternoon sun claims it from the west, to bask in the lack of green.

The crusty cold of late February will not be denied, but I cook oatmeal to prove the ice and snow can't touch the *real* me, the inside me. I forget who taught me to use wooden spoons when stirring oatmeal, chocolate, and other sticky substances.

Today, I'm with the disciples in their boat, Jesus asleep in the stern. If anyone doubts His humanity, not to mention how comfortable He was in His own skin, He provides this picture, snoring away in utter trust.

But lo, a storm assails the boat, and they fear being swamped. How long did they eye their leader, sound asleep, before taking action? How many furtive glances did they exchange, how many times did one of them clear his throat as loudly as possible or scrape his sandal against the boat's rough wood? But the Master slept on.

When they do rouse him, they sound agitated: "Teacher, is it nothing to you that we're going down?"

I'd like to have been there to see the look in His eyes. Mark tells us His instant reaction (4:39-41). "Awake now, He told the wind to pipe down and said to the sea, 'Quiet! Settle down!' The wind ran out of breath; the sea became smooth as glass. Jesus reprimanded the disciples: 'Why are you such cowards? Don't you have any faith at all?'" (MSG)

What answer could they give him? We picture them swapping baffled glances with one another. A few minutes earlier, the storm's wail prevailed, and all they felt was fear.

Now, because Jesus spoke a few words, everything had changed:

"They were in absolute awe, staggered. 'Who is this, anyway?' they asked. 'Wind and sea at his beck and call!'"

The storm's voice, the wind's wild scream, obeyed Jesus. Could it be that the voices assailing us obey Him, too? Could it be that having Him in our boats is enough, no matter what messages race through our minds? It was for the disciples, even though they didn't understand everything.

They gazed out at placid waters, shaking their heads. Then they gazed at the Lord, who was all they needed. As soon as they called, He answered, with power beyond their comprehension. Maybe the next time a storm beset them, they wouldn't panic. Maybe someone would remember that if Jesus was with them, everything was okay, and that at their cry, He would act.

This "crying out" is my weak point. Instead of crying out, I let the storm "stick" to me.

"It's just a storm," Jesus says. "Cry to me." But often, I don't, or I wait. Why? What is there for me in letting the storm whip me about? Why waste time in waiting to cry out to the only One who can still the storm?

Oatmeal doesn't stick to the pan if we use a wooden spoon, and using that spoon has become a habit. I don't even think about it anymore. Crying out to the all-powerful One to rebuke the inner gales that slash at my soul—that is my spiritual wooden spoon.

We know better than to think the winds will cease definitively during our earthly lifetime, but Jesus is in our boat, waiting for the sound of our cry. The goal is to internalize that safe space, to make it our reality. Sometimes our emotional backgrounds make this a gargantuan undertaking, beyond our poor powers.

The first three steps of the twelve steps address this dilemma: we *admit* that we are powerless over specific areas; *come to believe* that a Power greater than ourselves can restore our sanity; and *turn our will and lives over* to God's care. Ahh, to grasp this spiritual wooden spoon as firmly as I do my oatmeal-stirring utensil!

Peace

Chapter fifteen of John's Gospel burgeons with the word "abide" as Jesus teaches the disciples before His death. Our college Bible study group memorized much of this passage years ago.

"Abide in me, and I in you. As the branch cannot bear fruit of itself unless it abides in the vine, neither can you unless you abide in Me... For apart from Me you can do nothing" (John 15:4-5, NASB).

This teaching baffled me. How could I learn to abide? Of course, I wanted a blueprint, concise, black-and-white, and folded just so. I wanted to "do something" to obey the urgency in Jesus's words.

Now, in another season and time, I revisit abiding. Verses from Romans chapter eight instruct me. Paul describes life in the spirit as opposed to our old do-it-yourself agenda. With God's own Spirit in us, it's as if we breathe in rhythm with Him, once we learn how.

This model, more understandable when approached along with the concept of embracing God's action, invites our attention and participation. We stop thinking about what we need to do and focus on what the Spirit brings into our daily realm. We listen for His word and permit this communication from eternity to permeate our consciousness. Interruptions become the fodder for serenity. (Did I actually write that?)

Listening provides blessed relief from always searching for a word of wisdom to share. We relax as others speak, respond instead of reacting. We discover a new capacity for accepting disgruntled folks, taking note of what they don't say as much as what they do. In a domino effect, others' manners and postures may alter, too, in response to our composure.

We welcome what takes place before us and inside us without our instigation. We attend to that other voice, the beneficent heartbeat of an eternal message of grace and love. Our pulse gradually acclimates to that measured beat, bringing peace within and without.

Most miraculous of all, our stringent attitudes toward ourselves begin to change. The reality of God's viewpoint toward us deepens: we face our hurtful harshness toward ourselves and plead for a new heart. We accept our inability to produce such a change. No, all we can do is abide. For die-hard self-castigators, this is possibly the most difficult transformation of all.

At two, my granddaughter is all about "I can do it myself!" She strides with purpose through the house, making delightful pronouncements in her deep little-girl voice. One day, I sat by a campfire in the backyard as she carried a picnic plate with a hot dog on it. She handed it to me, I thanked her, and sharp blue eyes met mine.

Blond curls danced as she responded, "It's not yours, it's mine."

We laughed, of course, but how many times have I given something to God only to reclaim it? Abiding means the opposite. I lose my peace when I take back the proffered item. Abiding requires that I place it in His hands and leave it there.

"Abide in my love..." Abiding also means that if I blow it by reaching for what I've given Him, I go easy on myself. Perfection is the stuff of heaven.

The Still Small Voice

So what were we doing before when we thought we were "walking with God"? We read Scripture and prayed in the morning and throughout the day. We watched our Ps and Qs, careful to maintain our reputation as a good Christian.

We still attend to Scripture, and our prayers perhaps haven't changed that much. We ask for safety, healing for sick and hurting friends, help finding things we've lost, defense of our little ones, soldiers and volunteers, and guidance for government decision makers.

But we've awakened to the work with a capital W, the labor going on in our souls. My friend, a former Benedictine sister and now an oblate, describes this as "continuing conversion of soul." We may have acknowledged this process at times, but now we attune to it, paying attention with spiritual eyes and ears.

Daily, we unfasten the shutters, unbolt the doors of our spirits to listen and wait. What is our God up to? How can we embrace His agenda for us this day?

Earlier on our journey, weren't we concerned about what God was doing? Did all of our efforts amass only "wood, hay, and straw," as Paul says to the Corinthians, on the foundation of Christ? If not in tune with the Spirit, did we ignore Him, disregard His ministrations, allow busyness and activity to displace the embrace? This is a hard truth to digest.

Fortunately though, we sensed a need. During those early morning quiet times, we noticed a lack. Not able to pinpoint it, we continued to be faithful (or legalistic), but a longing encroached, a desire for more, although we couldn't say what. Maybe that's why I puzzled so much over the word *abide*. My entire spiritual demeanor countered the concept of abiding.

We've all experienced being ignored; it's no fun. But our

Lord watches and waits for our nervous bustle to calm. As He revealed himself to Elijah in a still small voice rather than in wind, earthquake, or fire (I Kings 19), He comes to us in privacy, on a landing of our own. We only have to stop, quiet our busybody minds, and listen.

He makes no mention of our past agenda, holds no grudge. His longing supersedes our own. Desiring our full attention, our deep communion, our embrace, He slips into our space and whispers the secrets we long to hear.

The Making of a Woman of God

Back during college days, besting Annie in a theological discussion was close to impossible, and she lived what she debated. Earnest, sincere, a magna cum laude graduate who learned later when she earned her master's degree that she had overcompensated for dyslexia all those years, Annie was an all-around close-to-perfect Christian.

And then the story goes downhill. Old voices spoke as she married Samuel, who had all the right Christian words but not the heart. He put on a good show, though, and Annie prayed, gritted her teeth, grinned, and bore seventeen years of hell on earth, true to her vows. But when Samuel's abuse of their children came to the fore, the truth began to dawn on her. She would say that *truth* became her word during those awful-wonderful years.

In one of her vivid childhood memories she stood in the bathroom, where her mother locked the two of them. Her mother lay in the bathtub bleeding, and she remembers looking into the mirror, putting her hands to her cheeks, and saying, "I know what I'll do. I'll go tell Grandma that Daddy hurt you."

Her mother grabbed her arm and stared into her eyes. "No. We never, never tell anyone about this." Forty years later, Annie still kept that vow.

But something about becoming aware of her children's suffering did it for Annie. She found help for them, and in the process, for herself, too. The "help" was about as much fun at times as digging up glued black goo from old floorboards, but Annie came out of her testing reinvigorated to live life not as she *thought* Christian women should—be nice; always put others first; joy equals Jesus first, others second, and yourself last—but with a stronger foundation in God's irrevocable, unconditional love and acceptance.

She came out alone, having faced down the "Christian" dragon that said no matter what her husband did to her or her children, it amounted to sin to separate from him. Certain pastors and churches took her husband's side and accused her of committing the unpardonable sin, but when he refused counseling and proclaimed he had done nothing wrong, Annie reached her decision, which brought the truth to light.

John Townsend states: "Sometimes setting boundaries clarifies that you were left a long time ago, in every way perhaps, except physically." For Annie, it was far better to face the truth and be set free than to cling to a vow her spouse had already broken repeatedly.

Who knows how many people Annie has helped since then? One woman, for example, had trouble standing up for herself with a bully-relative who enjoyed touching her a bit too much. She says, "This had been going on for years, and I tried everything—except standing up to him. I should have screamed in his face at a family gathering, 'Get your hands off me, you pond scum!' But, of course, I didn't want to hurt anyone's feelings. I was such a nice, patient Christian!"

Annie e-mailed her this real-life story one day. Seeing her situation in a new, realistic light brought objectivity to the situation and instigated a new perspective.

> *Let me tell you a story about what happened to me at work this week. One of the women I work with treated everyone to special aromatic flavored coffee. For reasons I can't fully explain, I get violently nauseated at the smell of coffee, and so I literally tried to choke back the heaves. Makes no sense, it just is.*
>
> *When I told her what had happened, her response was that she was so sorry, she didn't know, but she would never bring that coffee in*

again. Now, did I do something wrong? And the fact that other people will be impacted by my "coffee problem," am I to blame? Or do we need to blame?

The office now knows out of respect for me they won't do aromatic coffee. No one said that's just stupid and they will make it and I need to understand that "giving me special coffee" is the way they show they care about me, and if it makes me sick, there's something wrong with me.

Sometimes it's unwanted coffee. Sometimes unwanted hugs. Not much difference.

Sometimes our church life focuses so much on "all our righteousness is as filthy rags," we don't see ourselves as having any value, and so when a situation like yours, where someone "bigger and stronger" enters our world, we default to the "damned sinner" role and think it's always our fault.

But the good news is you are made in the image of God! And even God sets boundaries for himself. So bottom line, you are worthy to say, "Don't hug me, please, and I'd prefer not to stand next to you." Think about how he would respond, and practice saying, "That is really about you, not me," no matter what he says.

Because it's true. We mature a little more when we realize not everything is about us. The guilt doesn't always lie in our corner.

Coffee or hugs, we are who we are, and we have the right to make some choices of our own. We may feel out of our element for a while as we make necessary changes, but often a "new normal" is a good thing.

A Time to Refrain

Jesus said, "The first in importance is, 'Listen, Israel: The Lord your God is one; so love the Lord God with all your passion and prayer and intelligence and energy.' And here is the second: 'Love others as well as you love yourself.' There is no other commandment that ranks with these" (Mark 12:30-31, MSG).

The word for today is *as*—such a short, nondescript utterance, we rarely take note of it. But Jesus uses the one-syllable to show us how to love others, the second greatest commandment.

Holding up a hand like a stop sign to maintain an acceptable distance may seem like an insignificant action, too, but for victims of abuse, keeping any unsafe person at arm's length constitutes the very minimum of self-respect. Any empowerment we appropriate in our defense makes a statement concerning our progress.

Even the seemingly small act like holding up our hand often takes a great build-up of emotional empowerment. As children, abuse victims had no such power, and often decades of tolerating inappropriate boundary encroachment pass before they realize their God-given right to safety.

Our need for distance exhibits itself in various ways—trembling, heart palpitations, a sense of disgust or revulsion, or extreme restlessness in the presence of potential danger. Others may see us as "together," but put us in the presence of someone who senses and takes advantage of our shame, and helplessness takes us back to our childhood impotence against predators.

A female school administrator says: "Not only children experience this inability to stop boundary-abusers. A 'power woman'—someone others perceive as strong—may fight this battle, though appearing confident and in control. She acts like everything is cool. In order to not disappoint everyone, she pretends to deflect the bully's poisonous arrows pointed straight at her victim-heart.

"Think about it, why would she want the bully *and* everyone else to know her weakness—hurting/crying/dying inside from the abuser's attacks? If they did, the bully would win twice and make her seem like a double-loser. So, to the external world it may appear this victim is strong and unaffected by the bully, but in reality, she is still powerless to completely stop the damage."

If allowing others to tramp over our personal space, or pretending their encroachments didn't exist served us well as children, we must claim our personal power for our mental health. When our physiological alarms warn of childhood replays, hard work lies ahead. We must respond to our "gut," whatever the consequences.

The other person may ignore our anxiety, or even act hurt or angry when we finally attend to our inner urging. But we've learned the anguish of shushing this voice and have discovered its faithfulness. This voice wills us to be whole. This voice deems us worthy of our own personal space.

To onlookers, our response may seem selfish or stilted, especially when we have no choice but to avoid boundary abusers who deny the facts. (Unfortunately, these folks skulk in families.) Once, we would have owned their cowardice as our problem. As usual, the whole situation is our fault.

But we have come to view our own needs as equal to others'. We don't want to hurt anyone, and at long last, "anyone" includes ourselves, our first responsibility. At such a time, the two-word phrase *as yourself* becomes our word.

What may appear self-centered is actually hard-won basic human dignity, and when we name it, we claim our personal power. If someone shames or blames us, we simply withdraw, dignity intact. Our intuition is enough. We can live without the approval of everyone in our world.

All of our lives, we've ignored encroachments lest we offend or hurt someone's feelings. Finally we acknowledge that our feelings matter as much as anyone else's. Love your neighbor AS yourself. As becomes our word for this day. And there's another positive: when we claim our God-given dignity, others have opportunity to learn the meaning of boundaries, a topic the Bible addresses succinctly.

"Do not move an ancient boundary stone or encroach on the fields of the fatherless, for their Defender is strong; he will take up their case against you" (Proverbs 23:10, NIV).

"Judah's leaders are like those who move boundary stones. I will pour out my wrath on them like a flood of water" (Hosea 5:10-11, NIV).

The God who gave His only Son for us cares about property violations. Our shame-based foundations make it difficult for us to accept God's concern about our personal property in the form of our body and our space. Old voices shout that we are not worthy of our inherent dignity. Everyone else deserves their space, but not us.

But this basic human right—to be who we are in the space we're allotted—eludes us no more. Ecclesiastes details times for embracing and for refraining from embracing. What parameters help us decide what time it is? First and foremost, our gut-level emotions, then the other person's response to our honesty, however difficult straightforwardness may be.

Touching can express someone's caring, or it can feed another's ego. They know the difference. Clearly, if care for us motivates them, they will listen and choose to honor our autonomy. Perhaps they are too lost in their own egocentricity to even "go there," and that's their choice. Either way, we walk away free from the shame-blame game.

The bottom line is our well-being, no matter how others react. When we once choose to stand up for ourselves, a new window opens, and letting go of the past becomes possible. Letting go of shame and victimhood broadens us to selflessness, to exchange anger, self-pity, and blame for the cause of grace. We can finally forgive and move on.

Fending off an undesirable embrace also boosts our understanding of what the opposite means. A welcoming hug entails no stiff arm, no internal disquietude, a sense of utter safety, belonging and rightness, a sigh of joy and relief, and letting down inhibitions.

We can give ourselves wholly to our trustworthy Creator, who designed boundaries. God awaits our readiness to accept His everlasting embrace as beloved children formed in His image. This One wants only our good. Stepping with abandon into His proffered light and joy, especially in times of rejection because of speaking our truth, we hold close His every whispered word, His every tender thought.

Spring

Spring must be near, but we say that tentatively as the seasons flirt with us. Sometimes in April, the temperature rises only to the high thirties or forties, bringing cold rains instead of warm ones. People who have already toughed out a long winter can hardly believe afternoons still require coats and gloves. Haven't we suffered enough?

We wake expecting daffodils but sometimes find snowdrifts. A few years ago, I penned a poem at the sight of a newly arrived robin surveying the snow-covered ground for worms.

> Fat robin, standing in the snow,
> fat robin, would you
> like to go
> back to springtime's warmth in the
> lands you toured?
> But this is Spring's surprise, dear,
> and sometimes surprises have
> to be endured.

Then one day the temperature climbs from thirty-four degrees to seventy in less than twenty-four hours, and we sit out on our back steps, the sun bearing down on our pale skin as it does in summer. Stunned, we watch the freckles pop out on our arms.

Deep down in its center, a lavender plant showed fresh green growth when the snow melted. Would it survive the snow and ice? Once in a while during winter, I reached down to break off a little stem, and sure enough, the leaves still exuded their healing scent.

Dilapidated groundcover, brown and crumbly edged,

promises new growth from the underside. In a couple of weeks, we'll step outside to a blending of old and new. Soon, we won't be able to tell the difference.

Spring works miracles through rain and sun, cleansing and warmth. Tattered becomes fresh. Brand new crocuses, daffodils, tulips, and grape hyacinths brighten the world. How can they appear so unsullied and young, after winter's brutalities? They went underground, that's how. Their bulbs retained life, no matter how impossible the circumstances, or how deep the frost.

Spring visits Christians beaten down by the struggle. God's gracious Spirit melds together the weary and the fresh into beauty, just as new windows, a porch, and siding add charm to a plain old house. (All on our list for next year.)

> "When the old compulsions reign within us as they have for decades, when despair destroys all joy and courage, sometimes at that moment a wave of light breaks into our darkness, and it is as though a voice were saying: 'You are accepted. You are accepted.'"
>
> ~ Paul Tillich

We can come to accept who we are, as Tillich says, "with a merciful, divine love towards ourselves." All of our questions come to rest here. No one promises an easy transformation. Narrow-mindedness and judgment do not transform overnight into broadness and compassion, but we can move toward merciful, divine love for both ourselves and others. Imagine looking at our frustrating, repetitive reactions with this merciful, divine love. That's a beginning.

We can stop giving our power away. We can move from being so afraid to cause trouble that we paralyze our ability to think and act with dignity and to discern our Creator's personalized instructions. We can develop an inner defense attorney who stands against harsh judgments contrary to God's valuation of us.

We can refuse all forms of abuse, including verbal abuse, and that includes the silent treatment. (Silence when there ought to be communication wreaks more psychological damage than a physical beating.) We deserve better that this. We are worthy of communication.

We can learn what is ours to own and what is ours to shun. We can allow others to take responsibility for their behavior instead of taking on more than our share of emotional work in relationships.

In the spiraling heat of July and on into August, who's to say self-acceptance and mercy won't overwhelm our spirits with glorious flowers? Transformation comes imperceptibly—one day we glance out, and the daylilies suddenly bloom.

Once again I survey our old house. In a couple of years, maybe a lovely porch will circle two sides, surrounded by tulips, daffodils, and crocus. Airtight windows and sunlit spaces...what exists now in our imaginations will one day be reality.

If we can turn an ugly old farmhouse into a thing of beauty, maybe we can learn to laugh at ourselves. We can allow God to give us "beauty for ashes, the oil of joy for a faint spirit" (Isaiah 61:3, KJV). Maybe we can learn to love the weak, needy human beings we see dimly in the mirror rather than entertaining condemning inner voices. Quel miracle, to love ourselves.

My friend from Wichita would say a loving lifestyle is all about listening, and that sometimes means setting aside our time-honored methods of decision-making. One year, she had every intention of attending her grandson's college graduation in Chicago. Her son Mike, the graduate's father, also has a daughter who would not be able to join the celebration since she was in mandatory camp counselor training near Kansas City.

This grandma never missed a grandchild's graduation, but when she went to buy her plane ticket, an inner voice she had learned to heed cautioned her not to. "What? Hello? That can't be you, can it Lord?" Accustomed to discerning guidance after long years of tough lessons, she obeyed. But as graduation day neared, her whys continued.

That Sunday at about 2 p.m., she thought, *I should* be *there right now*. Just then, Mike called. Her granddaughter had fallen twenty feet on packed earth as she navigated a ropes course. She was airlifted to a Kansas City hospital with undetermined serious injuries. Could Grandma drive there to be with her? Absolutely.

We need to allow God to blend old and new into willingness to do His bidding, even when it collides with our own. My friend did, although she puzzled over God's plan in the interval. But en route to Kansas City and her granddaughter's side, she knew. She could say she had listened and obeyed against all reason and logic, and her story proclaims the beauty of such a life.

Lance and I walk around this old house that has seen so many internal changes during the past year, but we've only begun. We envision a wraparound porch, a backyard deck and courtyard, and dark brown siding.

The window replacement truck pulls up...first things first. Because of this small step, less cold wind will blow into the upstairs next winter. A lot more warmth will circulate. Piece by piece, with patience and perseverance, beauty will come.

Dreams

Frost—thick and white—laces rooftops and posts. Sunshine will melt it soon, but for now, it reminds us to reign in our dreams of summer. So much like snow, yet more of a temporary decoration, frost cannot abide sun. It's April. Surely, not too many mornings remain of this silvery coating that makes slanted roofs into slides.

Coerced by warmth, frost disappears. It will have its day again, but not until fall. Once summer comes, we'll make memories of all that is not frost, and *life* will be our word. We'll hear it pulsing all around us.

Slippery, soft shiny grass, lilac bushes drenched in heady scent, daylilies blooming against the side of the garage, yellow primroses grinning up at us. Lavender plants near the back door, sweet peas and wisteria climbing the fence, and some unnamed white blossom joining in for good measure.

For two children, this will be Grandpa and Grandma's house, lemonade on the front porch, playhouses in the tall bushes. All around the yard, robins create nests and songs and delicate blue eggs. Soon we will hear the twittering of baby birds, the pulse of life.

Dirt-caked toes, onions to pull, beans to pick, trips to the farm, fires to build for hot dog roasts, s'mores to eat, feet in the creek, summer days in an old oak grove. Embracing life, we'll forget the frost.

Books to read, curtains astir with pleasant breezes, afternoon quiet time with Grandma, dreamy days, strolls through puddles to the library when it rains. Cookie dough, steaming corn on cobs, fireworks, swimsuits on the railing, raspberry picking, pie and jam making. Firefly-catching on the lawn, baseballs to hit with Grandpa, and games to watch from bleachers, popcorn in hand.

Time to play. Time to breathe. Time to be. Our dreams revolve around this house and resonate with our spirits. We have so much for which to be thankful. Joy comes to us as our inner eyes open. When we begin to slip from the present moment into despair, that eye offers, instead of judgment, a simple suggestion.

Pause. Breathe. Consider. Remember.

End Note

Virginia, ear cupped to the dining room radio ninety years ago; her daughter Grace in rural isolation, her friend encouraging her to write; the lady with her never-baked pies; an artist pursuing her lifelong dream; Mom doing the best she could; my Wichita friend searching for lost things with Saint Anthony's help: real-life women inspired this book.

By wisdom a house is built. By wisdom our goals evolve as we listen. The words live within us, though sometimes many years must pass before we can hear and respond. Words radiate through our individual personalities, our little lives, and this is no small thing.

When spring overtakes winter in our souls, our language changes, too.

"When" replaces "if," and hope enters into the statement.

"I'm taking some time off" replaces "I quit." "I have to" becomes "I get to." "I choose not to at this time" wins over "I can't."

"I have a problem, this is difficult, I hate this" rephrase as "I'm challenged with this," or "It's a time of exploration for me. There are so many possibilities."

Saint Andrew of Crete wrote, "While I breathe, I pray." While we breathe, God transforms us. One word at a time, our days take on new meaning. We embrace God's surprises as we engage in life. We make mistakes in order to learn.

In response to the devil's first temptation after Jesus's forty-day fast in the wilderness, He quoted Deuteronomy: "It takes more than bread to stay alive. It takes a steady stream of words from God's mouth" (Matthew 4, MSG). What better description of the Divine word upon which we ruminate in Lectio Divina?

Our thoughts lived out become our offering, a banner for

women who will come after, just as women from our past beckon us to make the most of the present, to establish our houses through understanding, to allow beauty to fill the rooms. As we respond, God transforms us through both trials and joys. What more can we ask?

References

Frederick Buechner, Beyond Words: Daily Readings in the ABC's of Faith. HarperOne, 2004. p. 139.

"He." Words and music by J. Richards, R. Mullan, and B. Feldman. Published by Ava Music/Warner Brothers. 1954. Renewed 1977 Warock Corporation.

"The Ninety and Nine." Words by Virginia Cecelia Douglas Clephane. 1868.

Daily Texts 2006. Mount Carmel Ministries, Mount Carmel Drive NE, Alexandria, MN 56308. Used with permission.

Robert Frost. "The Death of the Hired Man" from North of Boston. 1915. Simpson's Contemporary Quotations, compiled by James B. Simpson. Houghton Mifflin Company. Boston. 1998.

Robert Frost. "Snow" from Robert Frost Early Poems edited by Robert Faggan. Penguin Putman. New York. 1998.

"For All the Saints." Words by William W. How, 1823-1897. The Lutheran Book of Worship, p.174. Augsburg Publishing House, Minneapolis, MN. 1978.

William F. Buckley, Jr. "Why Don't We Complain?" 50 Essays. Ed. Samuel Cohen. New York: Bedford/St. Martin's, 2004. 64-70.

"Be Strong." Maltbie Davenport Babcock. 1901. Collected and published by Catherine Babcock.

Rudyard Kipling. "Sussex." 1902. From The Collected Poetry of Rudyard Kipling. The Wordsworth Poetry

Library, Wordsworth Editions, Ltd. Cumberland House, Hertfordshire. 1994.

John Kirvan. That You May Have Life: Let the Mystics Be Your Guide for Lent. Ave Maria Press. Notre Dame, In. 1998, 102.

William Johnston. The Cloud of Unknowing. Doubleday. New York.1973, 146.

Madeleine L'Engle. Simpson's Contemporary Quotations, compiled by James B. Simpson. 1988. 5887.

Preaching. Quoted in "Sermon Briefs offer Sermon Starters for Easter Season." www.preaching.com/resources/from_the_lectionary/11563754/page201 .

Paul Tillich. "You Are Accepted." The Shaking of the Foundations. Charles Scribner's Sons. New York.1948.

Saint Andrew of Crete. "While I breathe I pray." Also from "Christian Dost Thou See Them," The Evangelical and Reformed Hymnal, l941. Translated by John Mason Neale, 1862.

Other Titles

If you enjoyed *Catching Up with Daylight*,
you may also enjoy these other titles
from WhiteFire Publishing

Mountains, Madness, & Miracles:
4,000 Miles Along the Appalachian Trail
By Lauralee Bliss

Listening Prayer:
Learning to Hear the Shepherd's Voice
By Joanne Hillman